Presented to

_____

from

_____

on

_____

The Catholic Children's

$2

BIBLE

5/2024

Written by
Sister Mary Theola, S.S.N.D.

Illustrated by
J. Verleye

Regina
Press
www.reginapress.com

Imprimatur: C. Eykens. vic. gen.
               Antverpiae, 28 Maii 1983

THE REGINA PRESS
10 Hub Drive
Melville, New York 11747
www.reginapress.com

Printed in China

ITEM# 15190
ISBN: 9780882710587

ITEM# 1519290
ISBN: 9780882711416

ITEM# 1519292
ISBN: 9780882711423

TABLE OF CONTENTS

THE OLD TESTAMENT

UNIT I

IN THE BEGINNING

UNIT II

SIN AND ITS EFFECTS

UNIT III

A SECOND BEGINNING AND ITS FAILURE

UNIT IV

THE TIME OF ABRAHAM

UNIT V

THE MAKING OF A NATION

7

THE NEW TESTAMENT

DEDICATION

A work of love

offered to God

for my good parents

who were the first to instill into me

a love for the Bible

Dear Child of God,

This book of Bible stories tells of a God, the one true God, speaking to man. It is a treasure. Appreciate it and read it often and with devotion.

Through the stories it contains you will get to know God and how much He loves the world and all the beautiful things He has placed in it. He loves angels and men more than all other creatures, because both angels and men resemble God. Angels, like God, are all spirit. Man has both spirit and body; his spirit is his soul.

All through the centuries of the Old Testament and through the long centuries of the New Testament, including these our own times, God in His great love has always cared for each human being, giving to each His wonderful grace. The Bible shows how God watches over man, every man, even you and me. If we will have it so, like the many people of the Old and of the New Testaments, we can think of God as a tender Father walking with us, watching over us through all our days right up to the moment of our arrival at the gates of heaven. If on the way we happen to offend Him, He is always ready to forgive.

The greatest and strongest force on earth is God's immeasurable love for souls. Why does God love us so? Because we are made to His image. He made us for heaven. He does not want us to suffer in misery and pain through all eternity. Think much about God and thank Him over and over for His special love for you and for all souls.

Sister Mary Theola

The Bible is God speaking to you. It is more than a book written by man. It is a divine book, having God for its Author. It is made up of a number of books which were written by inspired writers. God did not tell these writers the words they were to write. They wrote in their own manner of telling things. But God directed them so that they told the truths God wished them to tell. They were God's instruments and wrote under the direction of the Holy Spirit.

Through the Bible God reveals Himself to us and tells us our responsibility to Him. The Bible belongs to the people of God and therefore to the Church. Catholics should know the Bible well and read it often, so that they will learn to understand its message in the light of the teachings of the Church.

St. Paul says, "Everything in the Scripture has been divinely inspired and has its uses: to instruct us, to expose our errors, to correct our faults and to educate us in holy living so that God's servants may be perfect."

In the Old Testament God speaks to us through His prophets and the actions of the Chosen People. In the New Testament we learn to know the teachings, words and deeds of Our Lord and their meanings for the people of God.

Reading the Bible will bring us close to God. Saint Pius X tells us that the fruit and the reward of Bible study are spiritual delight, love of Christ and zeal for His cause. Saint Paul says, "Let this mind be in you that is also in Christ Jesus."

UNIT I

IN THE BEGINNING

The stories of Unit I are taken from the first and second chapters of Genesis, the first Book of the Bible.

With the events given in these first chapters, God begins to reveal Himself in the work of creation. First He made the earth and then He made man, who is God's finest handiwork. He breathed into man the breath of life and made him lord of all creation. He created for him a garden of delight in which there was peace and security. Living was a pleasure, free from toil, and according to God's original plan, man was never to know death. What is of greatest significance is that God showed Himself a loving Father. He walked with man and deigned to speak with him.

Through the story of the angels we get our first understanding of the frightful effects of sin.

Genesis 1

God, a living Being, all-sufficient and happy in Himself, had no beginning. He always was. Nothing existed but God alone. And then according to His plan, God's goodness broke out in a creative act and at that moment time was born. As the Bible describes this moment it pictures an unformed mass of earth, waste and empty, and darkness hanging over the abyss. And above the waters moved the Spirit of God like a mighty wind.

God said, "Let there be light," and there was light. God saw that the light was good. God separated the light from the darkness, calling the light Day and the darkness Night. And there was evening and morning, the first day.

Then God said, "Let there be a firmament in the midst of the waters to divide the waters." And so it was. God made the firmament, dividing the waters that were below the firmament from those that were above it. God called the firmament Heaven. And there was evening and morning, the second day.

Then God said, "Let the waters below the heavens be gathered into one place and let the dry land appear." And so it was. God called the land Earth and the assembled waters Seas. And God saw that it was good. Then God said, "Let the earth bring forth vegetation: seed-bearing plants and all kinds of fruit trees that bear fruits containing their seed." And so it was. The earth brought forth vegetation, every kind of seed-bearing plant and all kinds of trees that bear fruit containing their seed. God saw that it was good. And there was evening and morning, the third day.

And God said, "Let there be lights in the firmament of the heavens to separate day from night; let them serve as signs and for the fixing of seasons, days and years; let them serve as lights in the firmament of the heavens to shed light upon the earth." So it was. God made the two great lights, the greater light to rule the day and the smaller one to rule the night, and He made

The Creation of the World

the stars. God set them in the firmament of the heavens to shed light upon the earth, to rule the day and the night and to separate the light from the darkness. God saw that it was good. And there was evening and morning, the fourth day.

Then God said, "Let the waters abound with life, and above the earth let winged creatures fly below the firmament of the heavens." And so it was. God created the great sea monsters, all kinds of living, swimming creatures with which the waters abound and all kinds of winged birds. God saw that it was good, and blessed them, saying, "Be fruitful, multiply and fill the waters of the seas; and let the birds multiply on the earth." And there was evening and morning, the fifth day.

God said, "Let the earth bring forth all kinds of living creatures: cattle, crawling creatures and wild animals." And so it was. God made all kinds of wild beasts, every kind of cattle, and every kind of creature crawling on the ground. And God saw that it was good.

God said, "Let us make mankind in our image and likeness; and let them have dominion over the fish of the sea, the birds of the air, the cattle, over all wild animals and every creature that crawls on the earth." God created man in His image. In the image of God He created him. Male and female He created them.

Then God blessed them and said to them, "Be fruitful and multiply; fill the earth and subdue it. Have dominion over the fish of the sea, the birds of the air, the cattle and all the animals that crawl on the earth." God also said, "See, I give you every seed-bearing plant of the earth and every tree which has seed-bearing fruit to be your food. To every wild animal on the earth, to every bird of the air, and every creature that crawls on the earth and has the breath of life, I give the green plants for food." And so it was. God saw all that He had made was very good. And there was evening and morning, the sixth day.

Thus the heavens and the earth were finished in all their array. On the sixth day God had finished the work He had been doing. And He rested on the seventh day from all the work He had done. God blessed the seventh day and made it holy because on it He rested from all His work of creation.

This is the story of the heavens and the earth at their creation. Nobody was present when God created the world and man could not know about it, unless God chose to let him know. He inspired holy men to tell us the great, profound truths of creation in simple, imaginative stories. These stories were written only centuries after creation and were written in a style of writing common at the time of the author. The Biblical writer describes God as talking, consulting and resting. He knew that God did not do these things. God simply willed and things came into existence. But this manner of telling the story helps us to understand more easily the great truth that God created the world.

The six-day arrangement of creation is a plan the writer used, hoping thereby to impress Jewish people with the holiness of the Sabbath, their day of rest. God rested; so it was right that the Jews rest on the seventh day.

Again, the author had no intention, when speaking of a "day" to limit the work of any creative act to twenty-four hours. He just arranged an orderly way of telling us how the many creatures of this wonderful world came into being.

The story of creation is a story about religion and not about science. Therefore, creation as told in the Bible does not offend against science. It is true, though, that in His creative act God set masterful forces of science into motion.

CREATION OF THE ANGELS
Revelation 12:7-9

Before God created the world and our first parents, Adam and Eve, He created the heavenly world of countless angels. These creatures are pure spirits of beauty and power. They are more like God than man, because like Him they are all spirit and have no bodies. Since these angels are spirits they resemble God in certain ways, but are far below Him in

19

Creation of the Angels

power and dignity. On the other hand, they are far above man. Angels are brilliant in mind and have a free will. They live face to face with God and were created to know, love and serve Him. They are grouped into nine choirs; the highest among them are the Seraphim and Cherubim. The angels are messengers of God and each man has a guardian angel to protect him against spiritual and physical dangers.

Because the angels were given a free will, God tested their love and devotion. Not all remained faithful. Some willed not to serve the God Who had created them. These would not accept His rule and proved to be unworthy of the glory that would have been theirs.

Their act of disobedience created a division of mind among these heavenly spirits and a great battle resulted. Michael was the leader of the angels who obeyed God. Michael and the faithful angels hurled their rebellious companions into the depths of hell, which God created for all the angels who had not submitted their wills to His.

These fallen angels were never to look upon the face of God. The change was immediate and eternal. Misery of mind and eternal hell-fire was to be their lot always. Lucifer, their leader, became known as Satan. In the Apocalypse XII: 7-9, we read, "And there was a battle in heaven; Michael and his angels battled with the dragon, and the dragon fought and his angels. And they did not prevail, neither was their place found any more in heaven. And that great dragon was cast down, and the ancient serpent, he who is called the devil and Satan, who leads astray the whole world; and he was cast down to the earth and with him his angels were cast down."

Both good and bad angels are interested in man. The devil and his followers try to prevent the children of God from attaining their places in heaven. They are jealous of the people of God and use their intelligent but wicked minds to draw them away from God. Until the end of the world there will always be this battle of Satan and his wicked followers against the sons of God, but in the end we know it will be God and His people who will be victorious.

Creation of Paradise

THE CREATION OF MAN

Genesis 2

The Bible tells how God created the material body of man in a special manner. It says, "Then the Lord God formed man out of the dust of the ground and breathed into his nostrils the breath of life, and man became a living being." This is the Bible's way of saying that man is a living creature, created by God and enriched with a soul which is spiritual and immortal.

Now the Lord placed Adam in a garden, the Garden of Eden, which was to be his home. Eden, as it is described in the Bible story, was a place of peace, beauty and plenty, a privileged spot. In this perfect setting Adam enjoyed intimate and cordial relations with God. He learned to see in God a tender and loving Father. The Bible lets us know how intimate their relations were. It says, "They (our first parents) heard the sound of the Lord God walking in the garden in the cool of the day." It was a place of abundant material blessings. The garden was well watered by large rivers, and out of its ground grew many kinds of trees, some delightful to the sight and others good for food. In this ideal spot man was to be pleasantly occupied and to be supplied with a great variety and abundance of food.

Of all the trees in the garden, two stood apart as special trees. The one was the tree of life and the other was the tree of knowledge of good and evil. The tree of life bore fruit that was capable of restoring the vital powers of man and was destined to preserve man's youth· If he had not sinned, the fruit of this tree would have made his body immortal. He would never have known death. It was God's plan that after a period of life in the garden, man, without suffering the agonies of death, would enter heaven, there to see and love God for all eternity.

The fruit of the tree of knowledge of good and evil had no such wondrous powers. It was through this tree that God planned to test the loyalty of Adam. God gave just one divine command regarding this tree, "You may

23

freely eat of every tree of the garden; but of the tree of the knowledge of good and evil you shall not eat, for in the day that you shall eat of it you shall die."

While Adam enjoyed great privileges in the garden, he was lonely. He had no companionship. Among all the living creatures dwelling there, none was equal to him. God planned, therefore, to give him a companion, a creature of his own kind. But God wished that first he should clearly realize this need. So, after creating all the beasts of the field and the birds of the air, and making Adam familiar with them, God had Adam give a name to each. By this Adam showed himself ruler over all earthly creatures. Having named them all, Adam knew that among all these wonderful creatures, not one could ever be an intimate companion. He realized his loneliness.

The Lord God then cast Adam into a deep sleep, and from Adam's rib, He made woman. From man God formed woman. Woman is of the same nature as man; husband and wife form one being, and the woman is dependent upon the man. When Adam saw his companion he said, "She is bone of my bone, and flesh of my flesh; she shall be called Woman, for from Man she has been taken." The love of man for woman is a holy thing rooted deeply in the nature of man and blessed by God. "For this cause a man shall leave his father and mother and cleave to his wife, and the two shall become one flesh."

Here, again, we have the inspired writer telling us an interesting story about our first parents. We must keep in mind that the story is being told for a religious purpose and that it is most important that we understand correctly the truths this Biblical writer wants to teach us. In saying that God formed man from the dust of the earth, he does not mean that God actually molded a man's body out of clay. We can be fairly sure that the writer did not believe this. Neither did he believe that woman was really made from man's ribs. The truths that his writings symbolize, or we may say picture, are that God, through a special creative act made man and He made them male and female. He gave them what no other animal was given, an immortal soul which has the power to think and reason and love. He also makes it clear that man is dependent upon God in body and soul.

God put Adam into a garden. The location of this spot has, until now, never been determined. The ancients spoke of Eden as being "somewhere in the east." But where the garden was is not important, but what went on during this period of Adam's existence is important. Here man learned to know God. Here, too, man was given great spiritual blessings.

There is another important lesson to learn from this story. The garden and the two special trees with all their imagery and loveliness are simply a framework to bring out an important eternal truth. God had blessed Adam and Eve abundantly and gave them a free will and then tested their loyalty. He gave them one simple command. It meant, "In the day that you sin, you shall die." Now Adam and Eve may have lived in a garden. Whether they did or did not, we may never know for certain and it does not matter. But this we do know: just as our first parents were tested, so, through millions and millions of ways God continues to test man's loyalty. The fact always remains. To be happy, we must obey God's law.

The Fall of Adam and Eve

UNIT II
SIN AND ITS EFFECTS

The stories of Unit II are taken from the Book of Genesis, chapters three to seven.

From the beginning even to this very day, all living creatures of earth except man follow the laws which God ordains for their existence. But man, made to God's image and likeness, was given a free will because God wanted a devoted and free service from him.

Having been given a free will, man needed to prove his loyalty. The test came when Satan, an able tempter, introduced lying and deceit. Man believed the deceiver rather than God and thus rebellion (sin) came into the world.

Even though man sinned, God did not abandon him but promised him a Redeemer. Through this promise final victory over evil can be attained for everyone who accepts God's grace and uses his free will to serve God.

Sin and wickedness grew and filled the earth until there came a time when there was but one family that remained true to God. In mercy God saved its members but the wicked were visited with His justice. Of them, not one was saved.

THE FALL OF ADAM AND EVE

Genesis 3

Unfortunately God's enemy, the devil, who is known as Satan, was set upon spoiling the security Adam and Eve were enjoying. As we have seen, Satan was a fallen angel. He was clever, crafty and revengeful.

He entered the garden of Eden as a serpent and moved on toward the forbidden tree, determined to achieve his wicked end. Meeting Eve under the boughs of the attractive tree of knowledge of good and evil, he cunningly addressed her, "Did God say, 'You shall not eat of any tree in the garden?' "

Eve answered, "We may eat of the fruit of all the trees in the garden, but of the fruit of the tree in the middle of the garden God said, 'You must not eat, for the day you eat of it you must die.' "

But the serpent, being a liar, deceived the woman. "No, you shall not die," he answered her, "for God knows that when you eat of it, your eyes will be opened and you will be like God, knowing good and evil."

The serpent's answer caused doubt in Eve's mind and immediately she was annoyed with a great desire to be like God. She believed the serpent and doubted God's word. She ate of the forbidden fruit. Eve had committed sin through an act of disobedience. After her sin, Eve tempted Adam. He, too, like his wife, disobeyed and defied God's command.

A great change came over Adam and Eve. They lost their intimacy with God. Man's innocence was gone and his lower nature was no longer under perfect control. The knowledge Adam and Eve acquired was that of guilt and shame. Peace left their hearts and now they dreaded to meet God. They tried to hide from Him.

In the evening, as was His custom, God came into the garden to be with Adam and Eve, but they did not come to meet Him as they had always done. The Lord God then called, "Where are you?"

Adam replied, "I heard You call. I was afraid and I hid." God said, "Then you have eaten of the tree of which I commanded you not to eat."

The man said, "The woman you placed at my side gave me fruit from the tree and I ate." Then the Lord God said to the woman, "Why have you done this?" The woman said, "The serpent deceived me and I ate."

Then the Lord God said to the serpent, "Because you have done this, cursed are you among all animals, and among all beasts of the field; on your belly shall you crawl, dust shall you eat, all the days of your life. I will put enmity between you and the woman, between your seed and her seed; he shall crush your head and you shall lie in wait for his heel."

God then punished Adam and Eve for their part in the offense. Grace, by which man's soul was made holy and pleasing to God, was gone. God had threatened death as a penalty for disobedience. Death, combined with pain and suffering, was to be the lot of every child of Adam. Eve, and through her all women, were to be subjected to much suffering in their children. Woman's position toward man was weakened. To Adam God let it be known that his sin brought a curse upon the earth which would henceforth stubbornly resist his efforts. Only through hard and wearisome labor would it yield its fruits.

Eden was no longer a home for Adam and Eve. God clothed them and put them out of the garden. Holy Scripture closes the account of our first parents' fall in these final words: "The Lord God put them out of the garden of Eden to till the ground from which he (man) was taken. He drove out the man; and at the east of the garden of Eden He placed the Cherubim, and the flaming sword, which turned every way to guard the way to the tree of life."

As in the foregoing stories, so here, the author continues to use expressive imagery or mental pictures to bring important truths to his readers. The message of this particular story is most important.

Here we see the true picture of Satan under the guise of a serpent who speaks and thinks. The serpent tells an outright lie, and besides, makes evil appear good. He is the greatest of all deceivers. As Satan acted then, so he does today. He is still a deceiver. He lies and makes evil appear attractive.

Cain and Abel

The unfortunate fall of Adam from the elevated state of innocence to which God had raised him, was the greatest disaster that has ever happened. Intimacy with God and the privilege of sanctity and original justice were lost. They were lost not only to Adam, but also to all mankind. Before Adam sinned he knew only good and had never had any desire for evil. After his sin he knew good and evil. He wanted God, but because he gave himself to the devil through sin, evil as well as good was in his heart. And so the conflict between the "seed," the children of Eve, and the "seed," meaning the devil and his followers, goes on in the heart of every man. Those who conquer evil in their hearts "crush the head of the serpent."

The punishment of sin followed swiftly. The devil, the immediate victor, was put under a curse and doomed to complete defeat. Adam and Eve, too, as the story relates, received their due punishment. And then God added a note, a word in favor of our first parents. Adam and Eve could certainly not have understood the meaning of the Promise as we do. Very likely the most they realized was that God would still be their protector and would not abandon them completely to the wicked serpent. Only as man by slow degrees grew nearer to God, was the great Promise of good tidings made clear through the prophets. Christ, the fulfillment of the dim Promise, was to be made man.

Cherubim placed at the garden gate, made a return to it impossible. The flaming sword was a sign which showed that our first parents had been sent from Eden and from all the pleasures they had enjoyed there. The happy state of life they had enjoyed in the garden was definitely lost for them and for the human race.

CAIN AND ABEL

Genesis 4

Now that the pleasures of paradise were theirs no more, Adam and Eve found life completely changed. Daily they experienced toil, anxiety and pain and these afflictions were to last a lifetime. Hope, however, raised their spirits so that amid these bitter sufferings they could still look upon God as a loving Father. His promise remained. If they were true to Him, they would always enjoy the blessedness of His loving attention.

There came a day when Adam and Eve had great joy. A man-child was born to them, the first child born into the world. Eve said with awe and wonderment, "I have given birth to a man-child with the help of the Lord." Later came more and more sons and daughters. As years went on, these intermarried and greater and greater grew the numbers that peopled the earth.

The Bible continues with the story of two characters familiarly known to us as Cain and Abel who were singled out for our study and instruction. They were brothers, quite opposite in disposition and in the work they did. One had a good heart and trusted in God; the other was wicked and had lost all respect for God; one was a shepherd; the other a farmer.

Adam and Eve instructed their children regarding their obligation toward the Lord God and so it happened one day that both Cain and Abel offered a sacrifice to God. Abel's sacrifice of a lamb was acceptable to God. Abel's heart was good. Cain offered the fruits of the earth, but God had no regard for Cain's sacrifice. Cain's heart knew sin. Cain became downcast and was filled with anger against Abel.

God said to Cain, "What does this anger mean? If your actions are good, will they not be rewarded?" But Cain put aside God's gentle warning and invited Abel to go out with him. When they had reached a spot away from home, Cain turned upon his brother and killed him.

Then the Lord God called to Cain, "Where is your brother Abel?" "I cannot tell you," came the insolent reply. And then, trying to cover his guilt, Cain asked, "Is it for me to keep watch over my brother?"

But an all-knowing God could not be deceived. And the Lord said, "What have you done? The blood of Abel has found a voice that cries to Me from the ground. And now, cursed are you in the soil which has opened its mouth to receive your brother's blood from your hand. When you till the soil, it shall not give its fruits to you; a fugitive and a wanderer shall you be on the earth."

Cain acknowledged his sin, but had no sorrow for it. Despair filled his heart. He said to God, "Guilt like mine is too great to find forgiveness. I am cut off from Your protection and anyone I meet may slay me."

In spite of Cain's hardened wickedness, God placed a mark of protection on him. This mark showed that God's mercy was still open to him. He still belonged to God. God had said, "Whoever kills Cain shall pay for it seven-fold."

It is necessary to mention again that we must try to understand the stories of the Bible, especially the stories of the beginnings of man, according to recent studies approved by Holy Church.

We have always considered Cain and Abel as the immediate sons of Adam. They were sons of Adam, but only in the same way that we are all sons of Adam. The description of Cain and Abel as farmer and shepherd belongs to a period much later in the development of man than the time of our first parents. The mention of them simply links the advanced stages of sin to its source, the "family sin" or original sin which is each man's inheritance. This story makes true the words of Saint Paul, "Through one man, sin came into the world."

As time went on, fewer and fewer of the "sons of God" were mindful of their Creator. Most men were slaves to Satan and were bent toward evil. The story of Cain's murder and his consequent fear of the evils that would befall him after his sin, is a way of picturing to us how strong and unchecked was the leaning toward sin and lawlessness. Man was hardened in sin.

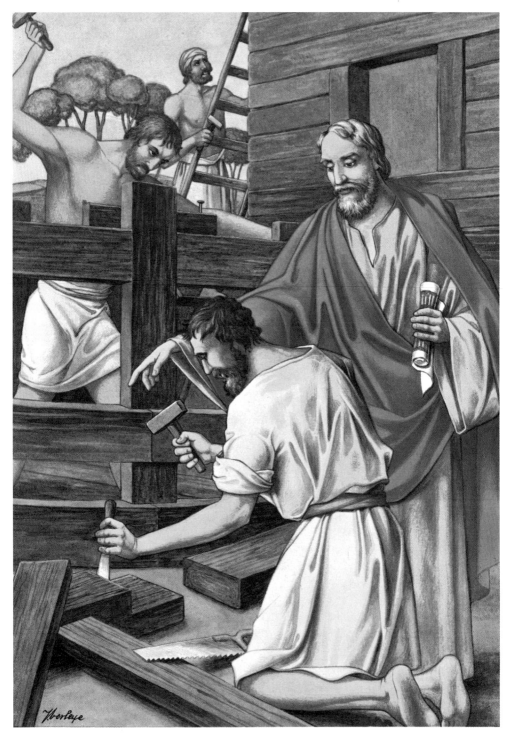

Noe and the Ark

Genesis 6-7

Noe lived many, many years after Adam. The period of this early part of the Bible was centuries long. The inspired writer divides it very simply into two periods, from Adam to the Flood and from the Flood to Abraham. He gives a few names of both good and bad and some scant facts of history. The one idea he wants to bring out strongly is the wickedness of man because of Adam's sin. Wickedness rather than goodness found a ready place in the hearts of God's people.

The record tells of an early material progress and gives credit to Cain and his descendants for building the first city, which very likely was but the centering of a few stone huts. Cain, it is said, named the city after Henoch, his eldest son. The number of men increased rapidly, so that crowded conditions and the raising of flocks necessitated a change in ways of living. The habits of nomadic peoples, peoples moving about and having no fixed homes, were established. The Cainites invented musical instruments and discovered how to produce and use metals. Moreover, Lamech, one of Cain's sons, made weapons for fighting which were better than the clubs and stones they were accustomed to use.

The curse put on these people because of their father, Cain, remained with them, and the sins of man increased. They lost sight of the ways of God and were irreverent toward Him. Instead of goodness, a spirit of vengeance dwelt in their hearts. They had no respect for human life; revenge was looked upon as justice. Murder and immoral ways of living held no horrors for them.

But God was not completely forgotten by the sons of Adam. There is a consoling sentence recorded in the Bible pertaining to this period: "At that time men began to call on the name of the Lord." Following immediately upon this statement is a chapter which names mighty men of the past, the fathers of the generations who feared God. Among them was Seth, who was given to Adam

35

and Eve to console them for Abel's tragic loss. He lived to the age of 912. Enoch is also mentioned. Because of his great holiness it was believed that the Lord "took" him from the face of the earth at an unusually early age. He remained on earth but 365 years. He is supposed not to have died. And then there was Methusala who was the oldest of all these great, holy men. He lived for 969 years. Saint Luke, in his Gospel which was written ages after these events, traces a direct family line from Christ through all Biblical history to these stalwart men, even to Seth and to Adam.

Now we come to the period of the Flood. Man had corrupted his ways. Of this the Bible says, "When God saw that the wickedness of man on earth was great, and that man's every thought and all the inclinations of his heart were only evil, He regretted that He had made man on the earth and was grieved to the heart." Then the Lord said, "I will wipe from the face of the earth man whom I have created — man and beast, crawling creatures and birds of the air as well — for I regret that I made them."

But Noe found favor with the Lord. He was just and blameless before God and untouched by the corruption of his age. God said to Noe, "The end of all creatures of the flesh is in my mind; the earth is full of violence because of them. I will destroy them with the earth."

Noe, his three sons, Sem, Cham and Japheth, Noe's wife and the wives of his sons alone found favor with God. Then God gave Noe instructions about building the ark which was to be their refuge during the Flood.

It may be well, once again, to renew our belief in the writings of the holy men who wrote the Bible. God, we know, spoke through them and in this particular story is warning mankind against sin. During these days preceding the Flood the writer's one intention is to show the growth of sin, and the awful truth of man's deep and hardened wickedness of heart.

Adam sinned and tried to hide from God. Cain's reaction to sin showed a rebellious heart. He refused to accept the responsibility of sin. Lamech, Cain's son, was worse than his father. Murder multiplied murder. Man's days became lawless. The moral ways of living, that means, the good ways of living, were entirely forgotten. Sin and murder and revenge went on increasing. The writer uses the lives of these men as a scheme or a way to show us what sin can do.

He uses another scheme to impress us with the wickedness of crime. To the Hebrews, a long life was a blessing and a short life, a punishment. So, during this period of sin, the writer makes wicked men live short lives while good men live many, many years. To the ancients, numbers were never taken literally, that is, for what they actually stood. They were only symbols and signs to help say what the writer meant to say.

During these days of wickedness there were some good men who give a brighter side to the story. These men were the sons of Seth and were known as "the sons of God" and they, the writer tells us, lived many, many years. But after centuries of human life God found that all men except Noe and his immediate family had become wicked.

THE FLOOD

Genesis 6-7

Wickedness had reached its fullness. In their lawlessness the wicked jeered at God. Blind in spirit, they may well have thought in the verses of the Book of Job XXII: 13-14, "What does God know? Can He judge through the thick darkness? Clouds hide Him so that He cannot see; He walks upon the vault of the heavens." But they were mistaken. God sees all things, both good and evil. And now, the day of reckoning was at hand.

God said to Noe, "The time has come for Me to make an end to mankind. I mean to destroy them. Make yourself and your family an ark of planks of wood. Coat it inside and out with pitch. Make it three hundred cubits long, fifty cubits wide, and thirty cubits high. It is to have windows and a door and an upper and a lower deck. I will send a flood over the face of the earth. You and your sons, your wife and their wives, and a pair of each kind of living creature, male and female, shall go into the ark. Provide food for yourselves and the animals."

Following these instructions Noe and his sons started their preparation for the Flood. It took them more than a hundred years to build the ark. The time of its building was the time of God's mercy toward His people. The building of the ark should have served as a warning of the tribulation that was to follow, but it provoked ridicule instead of repentance. Life went on as usual, and from day to day sin increased. The measure of God's mercy reached an end. God's justice would be satisfied.

When the ark had been completed, God told Noe to take refuge in it. And then, Noe and his wife and his sons and their wives and all types of beasts and birds and all creeping things, male and female of each, found shelter, protection and safety in the ark. The Lord shut them in and His spirit held them in safely.

Seven days passed and then the waters began to flood the earth. For forty days and forty nights the rain fell in torrents. The springs of the deep lying under the surface of the earth broke through. The waters grew deeper and deeper until they covered fields and homes and mountains. A seething tide lifted the ark from the ground unto its foaming crest. Without helm or rudder it floated safely over the wide expanse of swelling waters. The tallest mountains disappeared and the waters rose over them so that no living creature remained except those in the ark.

After the rain had stopped, the ark continued to float on the waters. God sent a swift, warm wind and gradually the waters abated, and land appeared. Suddenly, one day, the ark moved forward with a grating, grinding sound and settled on solid earth, on a mountain-side in Armenia. Noe waited forty days and then sent out a raven which never returned. After another seven days, a dove was freed from a window. It found no place to rest its foot and returned. Then once more after seven days had passed, again, a dove was released into the balmy air. It remained away all day, and returned in the evening with an olive branch in its beak. There was great rejoicing in the ark. After a period of seven more days, a third dove was made free to wing its way and it did, swift and straight into a cloudless sky and never returned. Noe then removed a section of the wall of the ark and looked about. The surface of the earth was once more beautiful to behold. Joy abounded. There came, then, an assuring word from God to Noe, "Come out of the ark."

Now again we have to consider the story in the spirit in which it is told. The author looks upon the story as a parable of God's mercy and love. A parable, we must understand, is a story often based on facts as is this one, from which spiritual truths are drawn. The truths on which this parable is based are that there really was a flood, that Noe built an ark and that he, together with his family, found safety in the ark. The spiritual truths which the story teaches are many. They are important and they are immortal. They are truths by which all men are brought to God.

Looking at God's part in the story of the Flood, we see His justice, His impatience with sin, and His holiness that cannot tolerate corruption. On man's part, the story shows the ugliness of sin, its rapid growth and the depth that human malice can reach in man. But there is a consoling side to this picture of sin. God's dealings with man are merciful. He allows time for repentance, and He does not condemn the innocent with the guilty even when the innocent are greatly outnumbered.

Confusing ideas have come up about the Flood. Was it worldwide? Were all the people of the world drowned? The writer says the Flood was worldwide. He, no doubt thought so. But the world was much larger than the people of those days knew. We know the Flood was not worldwide and neither were all men destroyed except those in the ark. Only the inhabitants in the area of Mesopotamia, where the Flood occurred, were drowned. The explanation of all this lies in the use the author made of the story. He knew about a flood that had really happened and told the story as he knew it. He used the story to teach religious truths. He was not interested in telling about a natural flood. The facts about the Flood may be questioned, but the religious truths, not. They remain.

The story of the Flood in Genesis must be accepted for its value of spiritual truths.

In the description of the ark, the religious purpose of the writer is shown again. His dimensions of the ark are fabulous. To him the ark had to be represented as gigantic as it symbolized or represented God's all-powerful protection. The ark is a figure of Baptism and also of the Catholic Church. The salvation granted to Noe as he was lifted upon the flood-waters, stands for the saving waters of Baptism. And the ark, even in the early days of the Church, was looked upon as foreshadowing it. The Church like the ark, is a means of salvation.

UNIT III
A SECOND BEGINNING AND ITS FAILURE

The stories of Unit III are taken from the Book of Genesis, chapters eight to eleven.

After God meted out His just punishment upon the abominations of mankind, Noe and his family, grateful for having been preserved from death, offered a sacrifice to God.

God was pleased with Noe's act of worship and made a promise to him, his family and to all posterity. Once more peace and harmony settled upon the earth. Man was given another opportunity to prove his loyalty to God.

But evil remained. Noe's youngest son made himself deserving of his father's curse. Through his offense and those of the posterity of Noe, pride and rebellion increased rapidly. Finally, filled with pride, this people planned to build a lasting monument to their own greatness. God's help was ignored.

The Lord, in His wrath against sin, stopped their work by bringing confusion on them. Disgusted, they formed into groups and scattered abroad. Instead of having a monument to their own greatness, they left behind them a monument to their folly.

The Sacrifice Offered by Noe

Genesis 8

The Bible says, "And then God remembered Noe." Warm winds came and the waters were diminished. Once more the earth seemed fresh and clean, and dressed in beauty and glory. In a spirit of reverence and with great hope for the future man again set foot upon the earth. Noe, his wife, his sons and their wives and all that remained of God's lower creatures formed a long procession as they left the ark.

Then Noe built an altar to the Lord. He took one of every clean animal and one of every clean bird, and offered holocausts on the altar. When the Lord smelled the sweet odor of the sacrifice, He said to Himself, "I will never again curse the ground on account of man, for the inclination of man's heart is evil from his youth; I will never again destroy every living creature as I have done. As long as the earth shall last, seedtime and harvest, cold and heat, summer and winter, day and night shall not cease."

God blessed Noe and his sons and said to them, "Be fruitful and multiply and fill the earth. Every creature that lives and moves shall be food for you; as I gave you the green plants, I give you everything." And then God continued, "I shall establish My Covenant with you and with your descendants after you. Never again shall all flesh be destroyed by the waters of a flood. I will set my bow in the clouds and it shall be a token of My Covenant."

As God pronounced His Covenant, a rainbow reflecting seven colors arched the sky. Kneeling before the altar of their burnt-out sacrifice, Noe and his family felt God's benediction upon them.

The history of the Flood was recorded by the Babylonians and other peoples about Mesopotamia. They enlarged upon the historic facts and told fanciful stories about the Flood. But the Biblical author, writing later, under the inspiration of the Holy Spirit, saw in the Flood, God's dealings with His people. He copied the facts of two stories that had been written and used them for his own purposes. That some points were contradictory

43

did not worry him and he did not trouble to explain them. Using what he had, he told his story about the great God.

In this story of a second beginning of God's efforts to draw man to Himself after the Flood, the holy writer tells of the everlasting Covenant which God made with His people for all times through Noe, His holy patriarch. God's mercy will prevail over His justice, He will bear patiently with man's wickedness, "for the inclination of man's heart is evil from his youth." God is merciful! And God's Covenant still remains, even with us today, a blessing in very truth. If God were to visit man with the full consequences of his crimes today, the world would be forever blotted out.

THE SONS OF NOE

Genesis 9

Now, immediately after the Flood, Noe and his sons began to raise cattle and till the soil. Cattle increased rapidly and vegetation was abundant. In the fall the grapes were large and plentiful and juice was extracted from them which in time fermented. Noe, not knowing the change which time had worked on the juice of the grapes, drank freely and became drunk, and lay naked in his tent. Cham saw his father thus and told his two brothers. But Sem and Japheth took a robe, and laying it upon their shoulders, went backward into the tent and covered their father; as their faces were turned away, they did not see their father's nakedness. On waking and learning what had happened, Noe cursed Cham. When he pronounced the curse he called his son Chanaan. "Cursed be Chanaan," he said, "meanest of slaves shall he be to his brothers." Then he said, "Blessed be the Lord, the God of Sem; let Chanaan be his slave. May God bless Japheth; let him dwell in the tents of Sem; let Chanaan be his slave." Many sons and daughters were born to Noe's three sons and in time their descendants moved out into wider and wider areas.

Noe was the one man untouched by the corruption of the age, but it was not so with his sons. The incident given above in the life of Noe resulted in blessings and in a curse on the nations to come. In the chapter of Genesis following this story the author gives a list of nations and a record of how the descendants of these three men spread "over the world." By "world" the author means the world that the Hebrews knew, the countries in a circle about the Mediterranean Sea and their own land of Mesopotamia. The expansion of these descendants of Noe was brought to pass according to God's plan through Noe's judgment of his sons.

The peoples who moved farther away from the surroundings of Mesopotamia are described as the descendants of Japheth. These were the "good" Gentiles whose relations with the people of God could be termed neighborly. From Cham (Chanaan) came those Gentiles who were enemies to Sem's descendants. The descendants of Sem had received Noe's special blessing and it was through his descendants that God made a second attempt to win mankind to Himself. Sem and his race formed a favored group and later they became the Chosen People. Noe prayed that Sem would always acknowledge and worship the one true God and that Japheth would enjoy earthly and spiritual blessings.

In the development of nations and their dispersion into wider and wider areas, what these men might have learned about God was generally confused and blended with other beliefs and religions, so that the inspired writer states sadly that even among the Semites many fell from God.

THE TOWER OF BABEL

Genesis 11

The story of Babel has to do with the descendants of Sem who migrated eastward and discovered a valley in the land of Sennar and settled there. They said one to another, "Come, let us make bricks and bake them." They used bricks for stone and bitumen, a black, tarry pitch, for mortar. "Let us build ourselves a city and a tower with its top to the heavens."

45

The Tower of Babel

"Let us make a name for ourselves lest we be scattered all over the earth."

The Lord came down to see the city and the tower which the men had built. And the Lord said, "Truly, they are one people, and they all have the same language. This is the beginning of what they will do. Hereafter they will not be restrained from anything which they determine to do." So the Lord scattered them from that place over all the earth; and they stopped building the city. For this reason it was called Babel, because there the Lord confused the speech of all the earth. From there the Lord scattered them over the earth.

In this instance, the author of Genesis uses the story of the Tower of Babel to show that man learned nothing through the punishments of the past. He is still sinful, proud and in opposition to God.

The original story of the Tower of Babel was written to explain the beginnings of different languages in the world. A tower was being built and a dispute arose between the builders and the workers. To punish them the gods confused their languages so that they could not understand each other and they dispersed into different parts of the world.

This was a mere story. In taking it over, the sacred author used it for a different purpose. He did not intend to explain the origin of languages. In chapter X of Genesis, he had spoken of languages, families and nations which had already settled the question of the use of different languages among men.

The writer sees something most offensive in the hearts of God's people and this is what he purposes to tell us. For Sem's descendants to have built a tower as was customary in the cities of Mesopotamia from mud bricks, no matter how high they might have built it, was not wrong. But their motive in building it was wrong. It showed the evil in their hearts and the pride of their minds.

The Biblical writer describes God as speaking, to show us that the minds and hearts of men were again turned against Him. "Let us build ourselves a city and a tower with its top reaching into the heavens. Let us make a name for ourselves lest we be scattered all over the earth."

This aim to reach a destiny according to their own planning, without God's help, is what the author condemns. A people living without the thought of God! It was the sin of Adam all over again. Man without God is doomed to destruction. And these were the sons of Sem whom God had chosen, with whom God had made His Covenant! They were not true to Him and Sem's descendants were rejected.

If the world was to be saved, it must be in some new way, for in man as a whole, there could be no hope. The author tells us that as mankind grew older, it became less wise, less righteous before the Lord. Then a new program was adopted by God. The promise of man's salvation would be carried on through God's choice of one man, Abraham.

UNIT IV
THE TIME OF ABRAHAM

The stories of Unit IV are taken from the Book of Genesis, chapters twelve to fifty. This unit completes the Book of Genesis.

Long after the human race had spread over the earth, God selected Abraham about the year 1850 B. C., because through him He wished to make Himself better known to mankind. God dealt on familiar terms with him and even visited him in person.

With this call of Abraham to be the Father of Nations, begins a definite historic setting of God's people. God wished man to find his way back to God. Abraham showed man the way by his simple but strong faith in God and his hope in a Redeemer to come.

The immediate followers of Abraham as leaders of the people, especially Jacob and Joseph, did much to make firm these beginnings: to put aside all other gods and adhere strongly to the one true God.

With Abraham the knowledge of God deepened and spread to other nations and so prepared the way for the organization of the Catholic Church.

God's Promise to Abraham

Genesis 12-13

Wickedness had again darkened the mind of man. The one true God was all but forgotten. The greater number of people were given to the worship of idols.

In great mercy to mankind God again planned a way to keep the knowledge of Himself alive. He knew of a virtuous man, Abram, living in the city of Ur. God's voice came to Abram, "Leave your country," it said, "and your father's house and go into the land of Chanaan." Abram had faith in the voice that spoke to him.

Even though he was not happy about leaving the city he loved, he obeyed promptly. Abram, his wife, Sarai, his aged father, his nephew Lot and his wife and many servants made ready to leave. They took with them their herds of cattle, their camels, and all their possessions.

God was pleased with Abram's obedience and shortly after made him this promise: "I will give you and your posterity the land of Chanaan. You shall be the father of a great people and through you all nations shall be blessed."

Chanaan from that time on was known as the Promised Land.

God blessed Abram. He lived in peace, was esteemed by his neighbors, and his flocks increased beyond all expectation. But there was a great suffering in his heart. Years had passed. He and Sarai were aging and yet they had no child of their own. Abram complained to the Lord.

The Lord understood Abram's sorrow, and one night God called Abram from his tent and said, "Look at the heavens. Count the stars if you can. Your children and your children's children will be as numerous as the stars."

Abram believed the Lord and was once more filled with hope. He now waited for a son.

Again the Lord spoke, "Your name shall be Abraham not Abram because you shall be the father of many nations. And Sarai shall be called Sarah, the mother of princes. I will fulfill My promise to you and give you a son. He shall be the father of nations and kings. You shall call him Isaac."

51

Melchisedech

Genesis 14:17-20

Because of quarrels which arose between the herdsmen of Abraham and Lot, Abraham suggested that their herds be separated. Abraham gave Lot the preference and Lot chose the land to the right, the land of Sodom and Gomorrah in the beautiful valley of the Jordan.

Later, warriors from the east made an attack on Sodom and Gomorrah. The cities were sacked and the people were taken into bondage. Among these was Lot.

Although Abraham was a peace-loving man, when he heard of the fate of his nephew Lot, and the distress of the two cities, he assembled his dependents and moved with rapidity to the northern extremity of Palestine to meet the raiders. His repeated attacks forced them to give up.

The victory brought great honor to Abraham. On his return march, the kings in the area who had suffered because of the invasion, came to meet Abraham and hailed him as a conqueror.

Among these kings was Melchisedech, the king of Salem. He was also a priest of the Lord and had come to offer a sacrifice of thanks to the Most High God.

A rough altar was quickly erected in the valley near Jerusalem. Abraham and his soldiers knelt in the hot desert sands around the altar while the priestly monarch stood before the altar and raised aloft a piece of bread. And then a moment later he offered a cup of wine to the Most High God. In this short act of worship, God's high priest blessed Abraham. In gratitude Abraham gave Melchisedech a tenth of the booty he had taken.

Melchisedech is the only priest of the Old Testament distinguished for offering bread and wine in sacrifice to God. There is mystery about this priest because he appears so abruptly and then never appears again in person, yet his momentary appearance carries with it a symbolism which will never be lost in the Church.

David, God's inspired psalmist says relative to this mysterious priest-king: "The Lord has sworn, and he will not repent: You are a priest forever according to the order of Melchisedech."

Saint Paul says of Melchisedech, "First as his name shows, he is King of Justice, and then also he is King of

The Cities of Sodom and Gomorrah

Salem, that is, King of Peace. Without father, without mother, without genealogy, having neither beginning of days nor end of life, but likened to the Son of God, he continues a priest forever."

THE CITIES OF SODOM AND GOMORRAH

Genesis 18-19

After long years, one evening, three young men arrived at Abraham's tent. Abraham welcomed them and Sarah hastily prepared a tender lamb. After the guests had been refreshed, Abraham sat down to entertain them. He soon understood that the Lord and two angels had come to speak with him. Abraham was overcome with awe.

When the heavenly guests were ready to leave, Abraham accompanied them for some distance. After they had been on their way for some time, the Lord told the angels to go on their way to fulfill the directions they had received. Then Abraham learned from the Lord that the cities of Sodom and Gomorrah, because of the wickedness in them, were to be destroyed by fire. Abraham pleaded for mercy for Lot and for the cities, asking that they be spared if fifty just persons could be found. The Lord was willing, but there were not that many just persons in the two cities. Abraham repeated his petition decreasing the number each time until his request was to spare the cities even though there were but ten just persons remaining. There were not even that many. Here the bargaining ended and the Lord disappeared. Abraham turned sadly toward home.

On reaching the city, the angels went to Lot's home and told Lot and his family of the disaster which was about to destroy the cities.

Early the next morning the angels and Lot and his family walked out of the city. As they went swiftly on their way, the angels warned them not to look back. Waves of fire flashed, and thunderous noise of falling brimstone rent the air. In spite of the warning Lot's wife looked back. Immediately she was changed into a pillar of salt.

Then and today, too, these cities remain a warning of God's just anger against the vice of impurity.

55

Abraham's Sacrifice

Genesis 22

God's repeated promise that Abraham should be the father of many nations was now made possible. Beyond all that could be humanly expected in their old age, a son was born to Abraham and Sarah. As God directed, he was called Isaac. Isaac was dearly loved, and Abraham knew that in him was the great hope of the nations to come. It was Abraham's great joy to see Isaac grow into a sturdy youth.

One night as Abraham lay sleeping in his tent, he heard the voice of God calling. There was no misunderstanding. The words were clear. It said, "Take your beloved son Isaac with you to a mountain which I shall show you, and there offer him to Me for a burnt sacrifice."

These words were hard to accept. But, nevertheless, at dawn, Abraham prepared wood for the sacrifice, saddled a mule, and set out with Isaac and a servant. After three days' travel they reached Mount Moria. Abraham directed the servant to remain below and wait there with the animal until his return.

Abraham took the wood for the sacrifice, bound it on Isaac's shoulders, and he carried the fire and the knife. Thus they climbed on. Isaac broke the silence: "Father, we have the wood, the fire, and the sword for the sacrifice. Where is the victim?"

Abraham replied, "The Lord will provide."

When they reached the summit, Abraham and Isaac built the altar and laid the wood for sacrifice. And then the victim was prepared. Abraham bound his beloved son; Isaac was made ready for the sacrifice. As Abraham raised his arm to deal the death blow, an angel stayed his arm. God was satisfied. Abraham had proved himself worthy of God's great trust.

God provided a victim. In the bushes closeby a ram was caught by its horns. Solemnly and with deep gratitude, father and son offered their sacrifice and then returned down the mountain and homeward.

Abraham's faith in God's word and his heroic obedience make him worthy of his title "Father of Many Nations."

Isaac and Rebecca

Genesis 24

Sarah died and was laid to rest. Abraham now in his old age had concern for Isaac. He called his trusted servant Eliezer. "By the Lord, the God of heaven and earth," he said, "I request you to go to the land of my kindred and there find a bride for my son Isaac."

Eliezer with a number of servants, ten of his master's camels and a variety of his treasures set out for Haran of Mesopotamia.

At Haran, when nearing the well of the city, Eliezer prayed thus: "Lord God of my master Abraham, the young women of the city will come to draw water from this well. May it please You that the maid of whom I ask a drink and who offers it graciously and, besides, suggests that she give the camels to drink, will be she whom You have chosen as bride for my master's son."

He had not long to wait for an answer to his prayer. A beautiful, modest maiden arrived and walked down to the well. Eliezer watched her with great satisfaction. As she turned to leave he said, "Kindly give me a drink from your jar." The drink was graciously offered and the trough was quickly filled for the camels.

At this Eliezer raised his heart in thanks to God. After the camels had drunk, he said, "Tell me whose daughter you are and is there room in your father's house for a night's lodging?" She answered, "I am Rebecca, daughter of Bethuel, son of Nachor." She added, "We have plenty of room for you and your caravan to spend the night."

Eliezer realized God's provident care still more deeply, for he was speaking to a daughter of Abraham's nephew.

Bethuel had died. Laban, Rebecca's brother, gave his consent to the marriage after Rebecca had been consulted. Rich presents were given to Rebecca and the family. The next day Rebecca and her maid left with Eliezer and his men for the land of Chanaan.

When the caravan neared the home of Abraham, Isaac came to meet it. There was mutual love between Isaac and Rebecca. Because he loved Rebecca, he was consoled for the loss of his mother.

Genesis 27

Isaac and Rebecca were married many years and had no children. Isaac, then, besought the Lord with great earnestness. His prayer was answered. Rebecca give birth to twins. The first-born was Esau; the second Jacob. Esau became a skilled hunter and was especially loved by Isaac. Jacob stayed among the tents and was peace loving, favored by Rebecca.

One day after they had grown to manhood, Esau came in from the hunt while Jacob was preparing a pottage. Being famished with hunger Esau bargained his birthright to Jacob for the mess of pottage.

When Isaac had grown old, he wished to impart his blessing to Esau. Calling him he said, "My son, go out on the hunt and when you have found game, prepare a dish as you know I like it; then you shall have my blessing."

Rebecca overheard Isaac's words. Quickly she called Jacob and told him the errand on which Esau had been sent. She finished, "Fetch two choice kids and I shall prepare a dish before Esau returns. You take it to your father in Esau's name and get his blessing." Jacob at first objected, but his mother's wish prevailed. Rebecca dressed Jacob in Esau's clothes and covered his neck and arms with the skin she had taken from the kids.

When all was ready Jacob took the savory dish to his father. "Eat, father. Here is the dish I prepared for you."

Isaac, who was then blind, said, "Your voice is that of Jacob. Come, let me feel your hands to make sure that you are Esau." Feeling the hairy hands and neck and getting the odor of Esau's clothing, Isaac said, "You are indeed Esau." When he had finished eating, he blessed Jacob making him his heir.

Jacob had scarcely gone out, when Esau entered with a dish of venison. When Isaac learned that he had been deceived, he trembled with emotion. Esau uttered a loud and bitter cry, "Father, bless me too," he pleaded. Isaac blessed him, but Jacob had received the greater blessing. He was lord over Esau.

Jacob's Ladder

Genesis 28:10-22

Rebecca feared Esau's anger, so Jacob was sent to his Uncle Laban in Haran.

At the end of the first day's journey Jacob rested, supporting his head on a large stone. In a dream he saw a ladder which reached from the earth to heaven. Angels were descending and ascending upon it. The Lord God leaned over it and spoke to Jacob. "I am the Lord, the God of Abraham and the God of Isaac. The ground on which you lie is My gift to you and your posterity. All peoples of the earth shall find a blessing in you. I shall not forsake you."

Jacob awoke. His heart was full of reverence. He cried out, "This is truly a holy place. I have seen the gate of heaven." He consecrated the spot, pouring oil over the stone.

Laban welcomed Jacob into his home. In time Jacob learned to love Rachel, Laban's second daughter. It was agreed that after seven years of labor he should have her for his wife. When the years were up, plans were made for the marriage. Laban, however, deceitfully arranged that the veiled bride was not Rachel, but Lia, Rachel's older sister. Jacob's anger was strongly aroused but when he remembered the wrong he had done to Esau, he quietly made a second offer of seven years of labor for Rachel's hand and so obtained his heart's desire.

After twenty years of service under Laban, Jacob with Rachel and Lia and with all their wealth, left Haran for Chanaan.

One night, while on the journey, Jacob lay in a restless sleep. A stranger appeared and wrestled with him. Jacob was strong and more than a match for his opponent. Toward morning the stranger said, "Leave me alone. It is dawn." He then touched Jacob on the thigh which at once withered. Jacob suddenly realized that he had been wrestling with a heavenly messenger. "Bless me," he called. The heavenly messenger blessed him.

Nearing Chanaan, more and more Jacob feared Esau's revenge. Through his servants Jacob sent greetings and gifts to Esau. To Jacob's great surprise and happiness they were accepted. Esau hurried to meet him. The feud was at an end.

63

Jacob's Sons

Genesis 37

Jacob had twelve sons. Benjamin was the youngest but Joseph was the best loved.

Joseph's brothers were already jealous of him and when he received a long, richly colored coat from his father, conditions became worse.

To make the feeling almost beyond endurance for his brothers Joseph was considered to be a dreamer of meaningful dreams. He related two dreams he had experienced. It was harvest time. He and all his brothers were in the field binding sheaves. Joseph's sheaf arose in an elevated position. The sheaves of his brothers gathered around his and bowed in homage. At another time he said that he had dreamed that the sun, the moon, and eleven stars bowed down to him.

This was too much for his brothers. They said among themselves, "What does he make of himself?" Even Jacob reproved Joseph.

Sometime after this, Joseph and Benjamin were at home alone with Jacob. Their brothers had been working in a distant field. Jacob sent Joseph to inquire of his brothers how their work was progressing.

The brothers saw Joseph approaching. Their jealousy was aroused. They said among themselves, "Here is our opportunity. Let us put the dreamer to death."

Reuben, the eldest, pleaded, "Do not kill him. Rather throw him into a pit here in the wilderness. Let us not shed his blood."

When Joseph came near, without explanation, they stripped him of his many-colored coat and threw him into a deep pit. Immediately after, while the brothers were eating, some merchants who were on their way to Egypt passed by. Juda proposed that they sell Joseph to the merchants. All agreed. They gave him over to the merchants for twenty pieces of silver. Reuben, who had in mind to rescue Joseph later, had gone away and was not present when Joseph was sold.

To cover their crime, they dipped Joseph's coat in some goat's blood and brought it to Jacob. "Is not this Joseph's coat?" they asked.

Seeing the blood, Jacob cried out, "A wild beast must have devoured him." Jacob mourned Joseph as dead.

Joseph Explains Dreams

Genesis 41

In Egypt Joseph was sold to Putiphar, the captain of the king's army. Putiphar trusted Joseph and gave him a position in his own household. Putiphar's wife became jealous of Joseph and lied about him. Joseph was cast into prison.

Here again Joseph found favor. The chief keeper gave him charge of a number of prisoners. Among them were the king's baker and his chief butler.

One morning both the baker and the butler appeared sad. Each admitted having had a bad dream.

"Tell me your dreams," said Joseph, "with God's help I shall explain them to you."

In his dream the butler saw a vine which had three branches. Grapes began to grow on the branches. The butler took the grapes, pressed them into the cup and gave the king to drink. The baker in his dream was carrying three baskets on his head. The topmost basket contained all sorts of pastry. The birds of the air ate from it.

Joseph gave these meanings to the dreams. The three baskets on the baker's head meant three more days when he would be hanged and the birds of the air would eat of his flesh. The three branches in the butler's dream meant three days also, but after these, the king would restore him to his former post. He would again present wines to the king.

Joseph asked the butler to remember him when he was again in the king's presence. Events happened as Joseph had predicted. The butler was overjoyed but soon forgot all about Joseph.

But God was still mindful of Joseph in prison. One night, two years after the butler left prison, it happened that Pharaoh, the king himself, had two dreams which all the wisemen of Egypt could not interpret. Then the butler remembered Joseph. When the king heard about Joseph's ability to interpret dreams, he sent for him.

The king told Joseph his two dreams. The king was standing near a river when seven fat cows came out of

Joseph Reunited with His Brothers

its waters and later there followed seven lean cows. These latter ate up the seven fat cows. Then the king saw a stalk of corn on which there were seven full ears. Then seven withered ears appeared on the same stalk and ate up the seven full ears.

"The two dreams," said Joseph, "have one and the same meaning. There will come seven years of plenty in Egypt which will be followed by seven years of famine. All that will grow during the years of plenty will be eaten during the years of famine."

The king was pleased. "You are blessed by the Spirit of God," he said. "You shall be ruler of Egypt."

JOSEPH REUNITED WITH HIS BROTHERS

Genesis 42

Joseph was indeed, a wise ruler. The seven years of plenty came. Joseph watched over God's bounty and built large storehouses; nothing was wasted. The granaries were bulging. When the famine followed, Egypt rejoiced. "Go to Joseph" became the watchword.

Egypt's good fortune was soon known abroad. So, Jacob, when his stores were exhausted, sent ten of his sons to Egypt to buy corn. Benjamin remained at home with his father.

Joseph recognized his brothers but they did not know him. He showed great interest in them and even asked about their father, and yet, he took them for spies. They were bewildered. Joseph kept Simeon as hostage until their brother Benjamin would come up to Egypt.

Jacob was grateful that they had obtained corn, but Simeon's loss and the thought of having to part with Benjamin later, were double sorrows to him.

Once more the family was destitute. Corn was needed, but the storehouses of Egypt were closed to Jacob unless Benjamin accompanied his brothers. Jacob remained obstinate. He would not part with Benjamin. Juda, after long urging, eased the situation. He pledged

69

Jacob Goes to Egypt

his life that Benjamin would return. Consent was given and the brothers started out.

When Joseph saw Benjamin he had to leave his brothers. He went out and wept. Later a banquet was served at which Simeon joined them. There was joy but bewilderment, too, over all that was happening.

Their sacks had been filled and now, reunited and well satisfied, they started on their homeward trip.

They had covered a short distance when officers on horseback reached them, commanding a halt. They were accused of having stolen the master's silver cup. Knowing their innocence, they asked to be searched. They were dumbfounded and disturbed when the cup was found in Benjamin's sack. Ashamed, they returned to Joseph's house.

It was Joseph who had ordered that his cup be put in Benjamin's sack. Now, when all the brothers were before Joseph, he said, "Benjamin, in whose sack the cup was found, will remain."

The anguish of the brothers was immediate and sincere. Juda cried out, "Take me. What will our father say if we return without Benjamin? He will die of grief."

Joseph could restrain himself no longer. He was convinced that now his brothers were of good heart. He said, "I am Joseph." Confused and repentant, they fell on their knees. But Joseph would have none of this. Joy abounded. Joseph had found his lost brothers.

JACOB GOES TO EGYPT
Genesis 46

Joseph was anxious to see his father and to have him and all his family leave Chanaan and come to dwell in Egypt. Besides rich gifts, he sent wagons for Jacob and his family to use on the long trip.

Jacob could hardly believe the seemingly impossible but joyful news. Joseph alive and ruler of Egypt! He could scarcely wait to see Joseph, but to move the entire family to Egypt, he hesitated. In his doubt, God's voice

71

came to him, "I am God, the God of your fathers. Go down to Egypt with all your family. I will be with you and make you a great people."

Jacob was full of joy now. He and all the family, seventy-five in number, moved south toward Egypt. At the eastern boundary of Egypt Joseph met his beloved father. It was a satisfying moment of intense gladness for both father and son, Jacob now an old man and Joseph in the height of his triumph.

Pharaoh welcomed Jacob and his family and gave him and his posterity the land of Gessen, a rich and fertile section of Egypt.

Here the Jews remained for several hundred years in peaceful relations with all the Pharaohs. They developed into a strong nation, numerically large. God was forming a people, His own Chosen People, the only people on earth who had a clear vision of the one true God.

Jacob lived at Gessen for seventeen years. When dying he blessed Joseph's two sons, Ephrem and Manasses, whom he had adopted as his own. To Joseph he gave this command: "Bury me with my fathers in the cave at Hebron in Chanaan."

Jacob blessed each of his sons but for Juda he reserved the greatest blessing, "Juda, you and your descendants shall rule over your enemies. The scepter shall not be taken away from you until He comes Who is to be sent and He shall be the Expected of Nations." This blessing was the beginning of the fulfillment of the Promise given in the garden of Eden. Genesis 3, 15: "I will put enmity between you and the woman, between your seed and her seed; he will crush your head, and you shall lie in wait for his heel."

God had indeed kept his promise to Abraham when He first called him away from his country and his home. Genesis 12, 2: "I will make a great nation of you. I will bless you, and make your name great, so that you shall be a blessing."

Joseph closed the eyes of his beloved father and had his body embalmed according to Egyptian custom. After seventy days of mourning, Jacob's sons and a great retinue moved in solemn procession toward Chanaan where Jacob's remains were buried.

UNIT V
THE MAKING OF A NATION

The stories of Unit V cover four books of the Bible—Exodus, Leviticus, Numbers and Deuteronomy.

Centuries had passed since the beginning of man. Man had increased to millions. Cities had been built and nations had been formed. In all nations, no doubt, there were some good people, people who in their own way followed their conscience and were faithful to God. But at large, there were no nations wholly devoted to the one true God.

During a period of almost six hundred years God had been preparing a people for Himself and now it was ready to be formed into a permanent nation. This group was to take the name of Israelites and to be God's Chosen People.

About the year 1225 B.C., in a miraculous manner, God's choice of a leader for this people pointed to Moses. Although the people he was to lead was God's choice among nations, it was seemingly not chosen because of its superiority in either spirit or culture. It had been a people suppressed through slavery, obstinate and weak. Only a man of Moses' unsurpassed powers of strength and leadership could have organized such a group into a united nation.

The great historic fact of this time was the giving of the Ten Commandments. These Commandments, given at this rather primitive time of man's existence, have come to us without change through generations and are to all mankind the fundamental blessing of a virtuous life.

The Rescue of Moses

Exodus 1-2

After several centuries the Pharaohs were no longer kind to the Israelites. The Jewish population had increased so, that Pharaoh feared for the safety of Egypt.

First he tried to reduce their number by working them to death. That plan failed, so he tried another. He issued an order that all male children born to the Israelites were to be thrown into the Nile River.

The persecution had now reached its height. God had brought the Israelites to Egypt; now that they were being persecuted, He would provide for their delivery.

A son was born to an Israelite woman. She managed to hide him for three months but to do so longer was not possible. With some hope for the boy's safety she placed him in shallow water at the edge of the Nile River in a covered, watertight basket.

As was her custom the king's daughter came to the shore to bathe. Inquisitive about the strange basket resting so peacefully in the waters, she had her maid open it. A child, a baby boy! At once the princess loved it and wanted it. Miriam, the baby's sister, had been watching. She lost no time. She inquired if the princess cared to have a maid for the baby. Yes, a nurse was needed. Miriam called her anxious mother. All things worked out well for the baby boy. He was named Moses.

After he had grown up, Moses was brought to Pharaoh's palace and given an excellent education. And under the guidance of his mother, Moses was also well instructed in the religious traditions of his own people. At heart he was a true Israelite.

It did not seem long until Moses had grown into young manhood and understood the sufferings of his people. He was grieved at the cruel treatment they were receiving. One day, witnessing the lashes given by an overseer to one of his fellowmen, his anger was deeply aroused. Moses struck and killed the Egyptian.

Moses knew that Pharaoh would be enraged against him. He left Egypt at once. He joined a caravan on its way to Madian. Here he lived with Jethro and later married one of his daughters. Moses had become a humble shepherd.

75

The Burning Bush

Exodus 2

A renewed and urgent cry for help went up to God from the heart of every Israelite. God was not indifferent to their sufferings and their prayers. Through these centuries of life in Egypt He had formed them into a people who were now strong in endurance and united in their belief in one God, the God of their fathers, Abraham and Jacob. The time had come to end the sojourn in Egypt and return to the Promised Land, the land of their glorious forefathers.

Moses was still living a peaceful life in Madian. One day, at the foot of Mount Horeb, a short distance from him, he saw a strange thing. A brilliant, flaming fire crackled in the midst of a thorn bush, but the bush was not consumed. Surprised, Moses wondered and then walked closer to examine it. Suddenly, a voice called to him, "Do not come nearer. Take off your shoes, for the place on which you stand is holy ground."

Moses realized it was the Lord speaking. He slipped off his heavy sandals, fell on his knees and covered his face. He waited in wondering awe for the word of God.

He heard the Lord say, "The prayers, miseries and sufferings of My Chosen People have moved Me to mercy for them. I will deliver them from the hands of Pharaoh and bring them to the Land of Promise. Go, therefore, to Pharaoh and ask him to let the Israelites go to the desert to offer sacrifice."

Moses was overcome. Without raising his eyes to the Lord, he cried, "Who am I that I should be chosen to do this work?"

God answered reassuringly, "I will be with you. I will give you powers no man has ever had."

To prove His word and to give Moses confidence for his difficult work, God had Moses change his staff into a wriggling snake and then back again into a staff. At God's word he placed his hand into his bosom. On drawing it out he found it was leprous white. God said, "Now

The Ten Plagues

replace it where it was and draw it out a second time." This time it was again normal flesh.

Moses was confused at the things he had done, but he had also gained confidence. He was ready to trust God.

Still there was one more point that bothered Moses. He reminded God that he was slow of speech. God appointed Aaron, his brother, spokesman and then was gone. Moses set out, the leader of God's Chosen People.

THE TEN PLAGUES
Exodus 7-11

As God had intimated to Moses, Aaron met him and the meeting was one of great joy. God spoke through the lips of Aaron, but Moses was always God's representative. When their joined mission was explained to the Israelites, the whole nation was filled with new hope.

Moses and Aaron appeared before Pharaoh to give him their message, "Our God asks you to let the Israelites go to the desert to offer sacrifice."

"I do not know your God. They cannot go, " was the curt reply.

After this refusal the work was made still more trying for the Israelites. They were not greatly disturbed. Moses encouraged them to trust in God.

A second time Moses and Aaron appeared before Pharaoh. Moses tried to give Pharaoh an understanding of the great power God had given them. In his presence Aaron's rod was changed into a serpent. Pharaoh was not impressed. The Israelites could not go.

Then followed a succession of plagues. The water of the Nile was changed to blood; frogs covered the land and ruined it; flies plagued man and beasts.

After the third plague Pharaoh and his ministers began to reason that perhaps this God of Moses and Aaron ought to be obeyed. Word was sent to Moses for the Israelites to leave Egypt. But as soon as the plague subsided, Pharaoh withdrew his word. His heart was hardened.

Crossing the Red Sea

Pharaoh and all kings were not a match for an almighty God. Worse things followed. Millions of frogs ate all the crops; swarms of mosquitoes pestered all living things; clouds of flies filled the air. At each new plague Pharaoh agreed that the Israelites could get on the march. But, when at the prayer of Moses the trouble eased, Pharaoh again changed his mind.

The plagues were becoming worse. Ulcerous sores sickened man and beast; locusts swarmed the land. And then there came a blinding darkness, so dark that it could almost be felt. No one dared to move. Results, however, were no better. Pharaoh's heart was still hardened.

These nine plagues took place at the word of Moses; they were stopped when he prayed. None of these struck Gessen, the home of the Israelites. God was about to send the tenth and the most frightful of all the plagues.

CROSSING THE RED SEA
Exodus 14-15

Before the last, the tenth plague, Moses called the leaders of the tribes together and told them how to prepare for the Passover.

On the tenth day of the month each family was to select a lamb and keep it until the fourteenth day. In the evening they were to offer it in sacrifice, sprinkling the doorposts with its blood. They were to roast the lamb and serve it with unleavened bread and bitter herbs. The meal was to be taken in haste, standing at the table, as they had to be ready to leave.

At midnight God passed over Egypt. His punishment entered every door not sprinkled with blood. The eldest child in every Egyptian home, from the king down, lay dead, so also the first-born of every animal. There was loud screaming and lamentation in all the land. Pharaoh sent in haste for Moses and Aaron and told them to leave at once and all Israel with them.

There was great tumult! The Israelites were packing and marching off! The Egyptians in fear even helped

81

The Ten Commandments

them to get away. They gave them gold, silver, clothing and other valuables, trying to make up now for all the misery they had heaped upon them.

The Israelites moved out of Egypt a free people. They were relieved but they knew well that a desert land lay between them and the Land of Promise. But the Lord was their guide at all times. He went before them, a pillar of cloud by day, and by night, a pillar of fire. The caravan moved south and was soon confronted by the Red Sea.

By this time Pharaoh regretted that he had freed the Israelites. He sent his army with chariots to pursue them and bring them back.

When the Israelites saw the army approaching from behind and the sea before them, they began to murmur and find fault with Moses. But Moses trusted God. He prayed for help. God told Moses to stretch his rod over the sea to divide the waters. And so the Israelites walked to safety to the opposite side over a dry path between great walls of water. With great speed the Egyptians followed over the same path through the Red Sea. When they reached its center, God told Moses to stretch his rod over the water again. The two walls of water rolled back over the path. Pharaoh's army was buried in the sea.

Moses and all Israel sang hymns of praise to God. Mary, a prophetess and the sister of Moses and Aaron, played on a tambourine. The women joined in with song and dance.

THE TEN COMMANDMENTS

Exodus 20

The march of the Israelites through the desert in the glaring sun was not easy. There were problems of food and water, attacks of fierce desert tribes. But in all these God watched over His people. Each morning they collected a white frost which appeared throughout the camps, a substitute for bread. It was called manna. When they longed for meat, thousands and thousands of quail flew into the camp. Moses struck water from a rock; another time at his hand, stagnant water became fresh and cool. A battle was won through the prayers of Moses. God was constantly attentive to His people in spite of their continued murmuring and faultfinding.

After three months they came to Mount Sinai. When the camp was settled, Moses went up into the mountain. Here God spoke with him. When Moses returned from the mountain, he gave this message from God, "I have brought you out of Egypt. I have taken you apart from all other peoples. I want to make you My people. If you will hear My voice and keep My law, you will be My special possession. You shall be to Me a Holy Nation."

Hearing, with one voice they responded, "We will do all things that the Lord shall speak." For three days the whole people prepared for the coming of the Lord. On the morning of the third day, as the people were approaching the mountain, thunder rolled and lightning flashed. There followed the sound of trumpets which grew louder and louder. God's presence seemed to light up the whole mountain. It was aglow with fire.

The people trembled with fear. They moved back, away from the mountain and cried to Moses, "Let God not speak to us lest we die."

Moses then moved up the mountain a short distance and spoke to God. The people could hear God's thundering voice speaking to Moses, but they could not understand. God Himself was giving Moses the Ten Commandments.

Moses returning, told the people all that the Lord had said. They replied, "We will obey the Lord."

The Covenant the Lord made with the people that day was inscribed in a book. A burnt-offering was made, and Moses took the blood of the offering and sprinkled it over the people crying out, "Here is the blood of the Covenant which the Lord has made with you."

The Covenant meant obeying the laws of God which included the Ten Commandments. These were for all Israel and for men of all nations and for all times.

Exodus 32

At the foot of Mount Sinai the Covenant had been accepted. Israel had chosen Yahweh as her only God. She would have no other. Yahweh in His turn would make the Israelites His people and protect them from their enemies as long as they remained faithful.

Israel understood the honor of being selected from all the nations of the world to be His Chosen People. When choosing them God did not in some miraculous way change their living to higher standards. They were still a people who had lately been slaves under the Egyptians. They were a depressed people without courage and culture and God knew it would take years to form them into a strong and valiant nation. But in spite of these and many other weaknesses He saw good in them and He would be patient.

Again God called Moses to Mount Sinai. For forty days and nights, without food or sleep, Moses remained talking with God. During his stay there God wrote the Ten Commandments on two slabs of stone. They became known as the Tables of the Law.

While Moses was on the mountain, the people below became weary waiting for his return. They wondered if he would come back at all. They gathered around Aaron and with great insistence said, "Come, make us a god who will be our leader; as for the man Moses who brought us out of the land of Egypt, we do not know what has happened to him."

Aaron felt powerless to stop the movement, and yielding to their plea bade them bring whatever gold they had and from their offerings he had a gold calf fashioned. They intended this image to stand for the one true God, and before it they cried, "This is our God, O Israel, who brought us out of the land of Egypt." On seeing this, Aaron built an altar for the calf and issued a proclamation, "Tomorrow is a feast of the Lord."

God was angry with the unfaithful Israelites. He had expressly forbidden them to make use of images in their worship. God said to Moses, "Go down at once to

The Golden Calf

your people whom you brought out of the land of Egypt, for they have turned aside from the way I have pointed out to them. I will let My wrath fall upon them and consume them."

Moses pleaded with God for mercy and so the Lord relented and spared them the punishment of complete destruction.

When Moses came down from the mountain to the camp and saw the people worshipping before a golden calf, he threw down the Tables of the Law which God had given him and broke them. Then he knocked over the golden image and ground it into powder. Moses asked Aaron, "What did these people ever do to you, that you should lead them into so grave a sin?"

Aaron replied, "Be not angry with me. You know well enough how inclined this people is to worship idols. They insisted and I yielded to their desires."

When Moses realized how obstinate a people these Israelites were and how prone they were to idolatry, he did not entirely excuse Aaron, but he understood his position. Then Moses went to the gate of the camp and cried, "Whoever is for the Lord, let him come to me."

All the Levites rallied to him and he said to them, "Take your swords and go up and down the camp from gate to gate and slay those who were especially guilty of idolatry, even those who are of your own family." About three thousand people were slain that day.

On the next day Moses said to the people, "You have committed a grave sin. I will go up to the Lord; perhaps I will be able to make atonement for your sin."

So Moses went back to the Lord and said, "This people has indeed committed a grave sin in making a god of gold for themselves. Forgive their sin. If You will not, then strike me out of the book that You have written."

The Lord answered, "Him only who has sinned against Me will I strike out of My book. Now, go and lead the people whither I have told you. My angel will go before you. When it is time for Me to punish, I will punish them for their sin."

Thus the Lord God punished the people for having Aaron make the calf for them.

The Twelve Spies

Numbers 13

When Moses was among his people once more, he built, according to directions he had received from God, the Ark of the Covenant. The Ark was a box covered inside and out with gold. The Tables of the Law which had been replaced were put in it. Then he built a tent of beautiful cloth to house the Ark. The Israelites now had a place to worship, a place where God made Himself present to them.

The Israelites had been away from Egypt about a year and were now in the desert just outside of Chanaan. Before making entrance, Moses decided to send twelve spies, one representative from each tribe, to scout the place. Josue was their leader. Caleb, like Josue, was trustworthy and strong in loyalty to Moses and his God.

The scouts moved quietly through the land and after forty days returned to camp and made their report. "It is land flowing with milk and honey," they said, meaning that it was an exceptionally productive land. Samples of fruits they brought with them were huge. A bunch of grapes had to be carried on a pole by two men. The people who lived there, however, were fierce and strong and there were a number of giants among them. The cities were strongly fortified. "We will never be able to conquer them," was the final statement.

All that God had done for them and all that He had promised to do was forgotten. The women wept and the whole camp broke into a tumult. They wanted a leader who would take them back to Egypt. They would have neither Moses nor his plans. Josue and Caleb went about the camp trying to make everyone realize that with God's help they would be successful. They made no impression.

God's wrathful anger was made known to them. He would destroy them and raise up another people.

"Forgive them according to Your great mercy," Moses pleaded until his prayer was heard. God forgave them but punished them nevertheless. With the exception of Josue and Caleb none of those who were twenty years old and over were permitted to enter the Promised Land. The whole nation had to wander forty years in the desert until all who murmured would be buried in it.

A Wandering People

Numbers 14

God's punishment was a great blow to the Israelites. But, in spite of such faultfinding and now and then falling back into idolatry, they knew Yahweh was their God and they were His people. They accepted their well-deserved punishment. They knew now that they would never reach the Promised Land, but their children would. This in itself was a comforting blessing.

The years spent in the desert was God's way of forming His people. The descendants of the twelve sons of Jacob under the leadership of Moses became a people. Their religion began with the birth of their nation at the foot of Mount Sinai. Its roots went back many centuries. The God who directed the Exodus was also the God of Abraham, the God of Isaac, and the God of Jacob. The religion of the Israelites was a personal relationship between God and His people.

Acceptance of the punishment to wander through a desert till death was readily made. But living these years, on the march, camping here and there, desiring better food, fighting marauders from time to time, often made the old rebellious spirit arise. Their ill spirit died hard.

Once when they were weary and rebellious, black serpents found their way into camp. Their bite inflicted a fiery pain and many died from the effects.

Moses was their recourse once again. They pleaded with him to ask God to remove the scourge.

God told Moses to erect a Brazen Serpent, and all who had been bitten and looked upon it would be healed. And so it happened.

Thus, the years passed wearily. Aaron was dead and so was Miriam, Moses' sister, and so were all the older folk. By the time the Chosen People neared the land of Chanaan, they were a nation of young, sturdy men. Through the mistakes and the sufferings of their fathers they had learned to trust the Lord. They were prepared to battle for the Promised Land.

The Death of Moses

THE DEATH OF MOSES

Deuteronomy 34

The whole nation of wandering Israelites had at last reached north of the Dead Sea, opposite the land of Chanaan. Moses knew that very shortly he would die. He was not to enter the Promised Land. God commanded Moses to lay his hand on Josue and transfer to him power and authority over His people.

Moses, then, with Josue at his side, spoke to the assembled Israelites. His prayer is called the "Canticle of Moses." In it he brought out the greatness of God and His power over all other gods and the honor that was given their fathers at Mount Sinai to be selected as God's Chosen People.

He strongly upbraided them for their weakness in being from time to time persuaded by other nations to adore false gods. He did not hesitate to tell them that he knew that their lives would not be different in the future. They would fail again and again. He told them of the punishments that would be theirs when they made themselves deserving of the anger of a God so holy and so powerful.

He told them, too, what blessings would come to them if they remained faithful. They would enjoy God's watchful care here on earth and His continued love throughout eternity.

After Moses had finished speaking, he walked to the top of Mount Nebo. From there he saw in the clear atmosphere, a magnificent view of Palestine, the Promised Land.

There, according to the word of Yahweh, Moses passed away. He was alone and no one knows his grave. There is a belief about him that though he lived one hundred twenty years, his eyes were not dimmed nor had he lost the vigor of his body.

Moses was a mighty figure. He delivered the Israelites and trained them. He established their religion, gave them a constitution, and made them a nation. His influence is felt even to this day in the Church Christ established. The Commandments that were given him on Mount Sinai are ours today.

Moses was close to God and a forerunner of Christ. The Scripture says of him alone that he spoke face to face with God. We must understand these words correctly. In the same chapter in which the privilege of speaking face to face with God is mentioned, it also says, "But My face you cannot see, for no man sees Me and still lives." The expression must be taken figuratively and means that a special knowledge of God was accorded Moses, superior to that given to other prophets.

UNIT VI
IN THE PROMISED LAND

The stories of Unit VI are taken from three books of the Bible—Joshua, the Book of Judges and Ruth.

Now that the Israelites were organized into a nation, God ordained that the land of Chanaan, which became known as the Promised Land, would be theirs. Josue, their leader, was gifted with military genius; not so the armies of the Israelites. They were unskilled warriors. But they had been assured of God's all-powerful assistance and they were given it. Their victories over the inhabitants of Chanaan were miraculous adventures. However, not until long years later, about the year 1015 B.C., could the Israelites rule this land with any degree of real peace.

Confident of final success, in the days when minor struggles to hold the land were still occurring almost regularly, Josue, under God's direction, divided the land among the various tribes of the nation. Each tribe was governed by elders, leaders among the tribes. And from time to time when conditions required it, God raised judges to instruct, correct and sometimes to punish His Chosen People. God was ever mindful of them, ever present with them.

The Israelites Reach the Promised Land

Joshua 1

Josue and the wandering Israelites had finally come close to the Promised Land. They were encamped in the land of Moab east of the Jordan River.

God gave this command to Josue, "Arise, take My people into the Land of Promise. I will be with you. I shall never forsake you."

Immediately Josue aroused his army into a spirit of combat. The Israelites had experience and were successful in the field of battle. But to capture a fortified city protected by massive walls as Jericho was, needed carefull planning. It needed skill and weapons which the Israelites knew they did not possess.

Josue and his council decided to send two spies into Jericho so that a scheme to strike at a vulnerable spot could be planned.

The king of Jericho and his people were alerted to all the movements of the Israelites in camp across the river. They had heard surprising tales about them and especially about their God Who had often saved His people miraculously and sometimes, too, punished their enemies. He and His people were to be feared. These spies, the king declared, must be found and put to death.

The two spies stayed in a house which belonged to a woman named Rahab. It was built close to the wall of the city. The king learning this, ordered Rahab to give them up. However, she boldly lied, giving false clues of their whereabouts. Meanwhile, the spies were safely hidden on the roof of her house under straw. When the soldiers were well out of sight, and night had fallen, she made her bargain. "When Jericho falls into your hands," was her request, "spare me and my relatives."

She did not let them go until she had this promise under oath.

After a safe release and a tramp back to camp, the spies gave an encouraging report, "The city is a bulwark of fortification but the people will not hold it. They are already in terror over the thought of an attack from people who serve so mighty a God."

Josue decided that Jericho must and would fall. The time was favorable and God would not fail them.

The Fall of Jericho

Joshua 6

To the Israelites, the Ark was the presence of God in their midst. They made the Ark the forerunner of all their attacks against the Chanaanites.

Set for the march to victory, the priests reverently lifted the Ark from its base and moved forward, followed by the army and all Israel. When they came to the edge of the turbulent waters of the Jordan River, Josue shouted, "Forward in the Name of the God of Israel."

As soon as the priests put foot on the waters, the waters separated and left a firm bed of dry ground. There was a loud shout of surprise and thanks from all the people, and with great courage they moved forward.

At their approach the huge gates of Jericho were closed and strongly bolted, while the inmates waited for the bombardment; but there was none. The Ark in advance, the whole people marched around the city in silence and then settled quietly in the outer surroundings.

When this same procedure went on day after day for six days, the king and all his people wondered.

On the seventh day those inside the city who were appointed to watch the doings of the Israelites saw the same march beginning once again. The watchers sat at ease but never surmised what was about to happen.

This day after the first complete march, the walk continued, around, around, again and again. Circling the city six times took almost a day. The watchers thought it amusing. The dust arose and the sun beat down. The Israelites looked exhausted and disheartened. Then after the seventh round Josue's voice came out loud and clear, "Face the wall, blow the trumpets, shout every one."

Immediately there was a change. All felt vigorous and alert. The air was rent with trumpet sounds and loud shouts. There was a quake, a rumbling in the depths of the earth. The mighty walls of Jericho swayed, cracked and fell apart. Israel's soldiers jumped over the fallen walls and began their slaughter. Every citizen was killed except Rahab and her relatives. Josue honored the promise of the spies and had arranged for her safety.

Josue warned the people to take no booty. The victory was not theirs; it was the Lord's.

99

The Conquest

Joshua 7-8

From Jericho the Israelites moved north to Hai. Confident of success, Josue ordered an attack. His soldiers were repulsed. This failure confused Josue and he had immediate recourse to God. Sin was the cause of their defeat. Gold and silver had been taken during the attack at Jericho. An investigation proved that Achan was guilty of the offense. He and his family were stoned to death.

During a second attack, by the use of skillful strategy, victory over Hai came to Israel.

Gabaon was near Hai. Its people feared the Israelites would attack them next. Three Gabaonites posed as wanderers and tricked Josue to make a promise not to injure them nor their people who had settled nearby. After the promise had been given, the wanderers revealed their true identity. They were Gabaonites. Josue was angry. However, he kept his word, but the whole people ever remained in a condition of servants to the Israelites.

Chanaan at this time was made up of both large and small states, each ruled by a separate king. Among them, there was almost constant struggle for existence so that often several states united against other states or planned a united front against foreign enemies.

So it happened that when the king of Jerusalem considered the success of Josue and the traitorous act of the Gabaonites, he was full of fear. He formed an alliance with four other kings and set out to beseige Gabaon.

A message from the beseiged city reached Josue. After a night march, Josue fell upon the enemies unawares. There was a great battle from which the enemy fled in confusion. They were pursued by the Israelites. As they sped through the valley, a storm arose and large hail stones killed many in their flight. The battle could not be completed, the sun was already well beyond the zenith. At the prayer of Josue the sun and moon stood still and prolonged the day for the victorious Israelites.

After this victory, Josue conquered the whole of Palestine and now he decided that the time to divide the Promised Land had come.

The Division of the Promised Land

Joshua 13

The conquest was not at all settled. Progress had been made and the Chanaanites realized that the Israelites had come to make Chanaan their home.

Bitter experience had taught them that it was a hard matter to fight against this people and their God. Open battles for the whole nation were at an end, but each tribe, depending upon the circumstances of its surroundings, had much to contend with before its families could settle down to a peaceful, rural existence.

Israel as a nation began with the sons of Jacob. The whole nation was divided into tribes, each stemming from one of Jacob's twelve sons.

And now Josue ordered the tribes to separate according to the plan which Moses had arranged for them. Some were to settle east of the Jordan, others in the northern hill country and still others in the central plains and toward the south. Juda settled in the latter section, and Benjamin's territory was adjacent to Juda's. The placement of these two tribes plays an important role in Jewish history. Christ was born of the tribe of Juda.

Josue had to urge the tribes to go into their assigned areas, for it was a difficult problem to take these territories over. None could enter any place with a feeling that they were welcome. The tribe of Juda was the only one which managed to establish itself strongly. After some years, the Chanaanites in this area practically disappeared.

There was a great change in their domestic life. Until now, through all the years of the desert, they had lived the lives of nomads. This new life required skills which had to be developed. Tents were discarded and houses had to be built. Fruits and vegetables and grains had to be raised. Crafts in gold, silver and weaving had to be learned and businesses organized. War was forgotten and homes established.

Gideon

Josue's work was finished. Just before the end came, he called together the princes and leaders of all the tribes. He reminded them of the great favors Yahweh had shown them especially in selecting them to be His Chosen People. He urged them always to be true to the Great Commandments Moses had received on Mount Sinai. He warned them against following pagan customs. A little later Josue died, at the age of one hundred and ten.

GIDEON

Judges 6

After the death of Josue, each tribe was governed by its own leader. As time went on, temptation came. Pagan neighbors had become friends and with them many Israelites took part in false worship.

When their sins became grave, Yahweh punished them. Usually, the punishment was an uprising against them by some unfriendly nation. When they repented, Yahweh helped them. He selected an individual from amongst them to whom He gave special powers to overcome the evil that threatened. These individuals were known as judges.

At one time the Madianites came down upon the Israelites and struck them with terror. God prepared Gideon, a young man of the tribe of Manasses, to overcome the foe.

Gideon's first test was to destroy his father's altar to the god Baal. During the night, following the vision of an angel, he destroyed the altar and erected one to Yahweh. The next day there was a great uproar in the village and Gideon's death was demanded. His father, knowing his son had done right, quieted the tumult saying, "Since my son gave offense to Baal, let the god Baal punish him." And so Gideon's life was spared.

There was a still greater work for Gideon. Gideon felt unequal to it but God assured him that all would work out well.

Samson

The Madianites by now had advanced and were ready for attack. Gideon assembled a large army to rout them. God had him reduce the number of his soldiers until there were but three hundred. To each of these, according to God's direction, Gideon gave a trumpet and a pitcher in which was hidden a lighted torch.

During the night when the camp was deep in sleep, Gideon and his three hundred men silently made their way and surrounded the enemy. When all was set, Gideon gave a blast on his trumpet. Instantly there was a prolonged trumpet blast from each soldier and at the same moment the pitchers were broken exposing a flaring, blinding flame. The noise and the sudden light in the darkness bewildered the soldiers. There was a dash for arms and the Madianites lashed out, brutally killing many of their own men. Those that survived ran from camp and never returned.

Now the Israelites wanted to make Gideon king but he refused saying, "Neither will I nor my sons rule over you. Yahweh shall rule over you."

SAMSON
Judges 13-14

The Israelites had been unfaithful again, and for forty years they were left to the mercy of the Philistines.

After that time God planned to deliver them. He sent an angel to the wife of Manoe of the tribe of Dan to tell her that the son she was about to bear would be gifted with great strength. He was destined to strike the first blow that was to weaken the Philistines.

And so it happened. Samson was gifted for God's glory with extraordinary strength. Once a lion crossed his path. With his hands, he tore it to pieces.

When he grew to manhood, he became involved with the Philistines and lost no opportunity to use his strength against them. He killed many in combat, singlehanded. Once, with the jawbone of an ass as a weapon, he slew

Ruth

a thousand men. Their crops of a whole year were burnt through another feat of his. At Gaza, he walked up a nearby mountain with the city gates.

Though Samson hated the Philistines, he did fall in love with Dalila, a Philistine maiden. This was sinful because he disobeyed God and Yahweh was no longer pleased with him.

Five Philistine magistrates came to Dalila. They bribed her to find out from Samson in what lay the source of his strength. Samson kept his secret for a long time but in the end yielded to Dalila's insistence. He admitted that his strength lay in his hair.

That night, while he slept, his head was shorn and his strength left him. The Philistines came, paid Dalila, and took their prisoner. After blinding him, they put him to work at a mill.

In his disgrace, Samson turned once more to Yahweh. And so it happened that when at a feast in honor of the god Dagon, he was brought into the banquet hall to be made sport of, he prayed to the Lord, "Return to me my strength and I will destroy this enemy." He then put his strength to the pillars supporting the building. They cracked, crumbled, and the structure fell. All who were in the building and Samson, too, met death.

Samson had faith and knew how to pray. He had made many mistakes, but his people loved him. They buried him in the tomb with his mother.

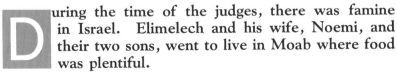

RUTH

Ruth

During the time of the judges, there was famine in Israel. Elimelech and his wife, Noemi, and their two sons, went to live in Moab where food was plentiful.

After Elimelech's death, Noemi continued to live in Moab because her two sons had married maidens of that land, Orpha and Ruth.

A great misfortune came to Orpha and Ruth. Both their husbands died. Noemi now longed to go back to her own homeland. She said to her daughters-in-law, "Go back to your fathers. May you each find a husband. Marry and be happy. I will go back to my own people."

Orpha kissed Noemi farewell but Ruth pleaded not to be left behind. "Do not ask me to leave you," she said. "Wherever you go, I shall go. Your people shall be my people. And your God shall be my God."

So, Noemi and Ruth came to Juda. They were very poor. It was the time of the harvest and Ruth offered to glean barley in the fields.

Not knowing, Ruth went to glean in the fields of Booz, a kinsman of her deceased husband. Neither did Booz know Ruth. He saw her gentleness and later learned that she was daughter-in-law to Noemi. He showed Ruth great kindness and invited her to continue to glean in his fields.

After making certain of the facts regarding Ruth, he married her. There was a law among the Israelites by which the nearest relative of a man who died childless, should marry his widow.

Ruth was happy with Booz and Noemi remained to live with them.

Ruth became the mother of Obed who was the grandfather of King David. And it was from David's line that Christ was born. So, even though Ruth was an Israelite only by adoption, God's blessing was hers abundantly.

UNIT VII

ISRAEL RULED BY KINGS

The stories of Unit VII are taken from the Books of Kings.

The Israelites finally settled in a land which they could call their own, but it was a problem to hold this land against the Philistines who were a united nation and were better equipped in military warfare. The loose confederation of the tribes of Israel did not give them national strength. At this time, a kingship for Israel seemed a necessity.

The desire for a king, though, did not arise entirely from the need for one. Except for the elders and military leaders, the great majority of the Israelites wanted a king merely that they might appear to be on a like social standing with other nations. This desire was wrong and showed ingratitude to God Who had always been revered as their King, and through His divine guidance had brought them from bondage to liberty.

For this reason Samuel, the judge at this time, was reluctant to comply with their request. After long, serious reflection and after he had become certain that the Lord God wanted His Chosen People to have a king, he found a king for them in the person of Saul.

Never in Israel was the will of the king the supreme law of the land. God's will was to be accomplished and to that end God worked through the kings. But when the kings made themselves deserving of correction or of chastisement, the Lord raised up prophets who stood for God against the king.

Samuel

1 Samuel 3

Heli became judge and exercised the office of high priest at Shiloh where the Ark had found a resting place. As Heli grew older he was forced to depend upon his two sons, Ophni and Phinees. Unlike their father, they were unfaithful in the service of the Lord. Heli rebuked them mildly but did nothing more to put a stop to their wickedness. Yahweh was displeased and sent a messenger who warned Heli that misfortune would come to him, to his sons, and to his kinsmen.

In the meantime Yahweh, mindful of His people, planned to give them another spiritual leader. Elcana and Anna had besought the Lord for years for a child. Their prayers were answered in the gift of a son whom they named Samuel. Even though Samuel was her joy, when he reached an age at which he could be away from his mother, Anna offered him to the service of Yahweh. He ministered to Heli in the temple at Shiloh.

One night, when Samuel was still a mere boy, he heard in sleep a voice calling him. Thinking it to be Heli, he went to him only to learn that Heli had not called. This happened a second and third time.

"It must be the Lord," said Heli. "Should the voice call again say, 'Speak, Lord, for Thy servant heareth!'" And so it happened. The Lord told Samuel that soon the threats which He had made known to Heli would come upon him, his sons, and all his family.

When Samuel told Heli the Lord's message, Heli bowed his head submissively to God's holy will.

Quickly chastisement came. The Philistines mustered their forces against the Israelites. After the Israelites had suffered a severe loss, the elders requested that the Ark be carried into battle. It was brought by Heli's sons. The sight of it uplifted the army's hopes for victory. Actually though, the battle told a different story. Thirty thousand Israelites were slain, among them the two sons of Heli. And besides, the Philistines captured the Ark.

A runner brought Heli the news. Hearing it, he fell backward, dead. And so the measure of God's threat was carried out.

Samuel grew up enjoying the favor of the Lord. No word he spoke went unfulfilled so that his favor was sought through all Israel. After the first revelation of the Lord concerning Heli, there were many more. Through Samuel God remained close to His people, and when Samuel spoke all Israel listened.

Now the Philistines had the Ark and kept it seven months. During that time it was moved from city to city because wherever it rested plague and public disorder resulted. Finally, after consultation with the Philistine pagan priests and diviners, the rulers returned the Ark with a gift in reparation for their disrespect toward the God of Israel. The Ark and the gift were put on a newly made wagon drawn by two heifers. Without a guide the heifers walked along on the road leading to Israel. Israel rejoiced at the return of its sacred Ark, especially because of the manner in which it was sent. Their Ark was respected.

With the Ark in their midst once more, hopes arose. "Now we will defeat our enemy," they thought. But it was not so. Every attempt failed. Samuel came out strongly and told them why they were not succeeding. Living among idolatrous people, many followed the religious practices of their neighbors.

"Your faith in Yahweh has become weak," he told them. "Faith must be renewed. Put aside all false gods and pray to Yahweh alone. Only then will you be blessed with the power to overcome your enemies." Samuel proposed a day of fasting, prayer and repentance at Masphath. Fervor revived and on the day of penance all roads to Masphath were crowded.

When the Philistines heard of the mass assembly at Masphath, their chiefs with a large army came in haste to give the Israelites a surprise attack. The Israelites were unprepared and became full of fear. But fear had a good effect. Now, helpless, they looked to Yahweh for help. Their situation spurred them on to trust.

Samuel and all the people who did not meet the enemy remained at prayer. The fighting group marched on with great courage. Their spirit had returned.

As the invading army neared Masphath, suddenly, the skies volleyed terrific thunder, lightning and heavy rains against them. The crashes were tremendous and continuous. The army became confused and fell before the onslaught of the Israelites. After this miraculous help the Philistines dared not attack the Israelites for a long time.

It is quite possible that had the Israelites continued to be loyal to Yahweh, their struggles to gain the land God had promised them through Abraham, would have been greatly lessened. Yet they had made progress and now during the closing years of Samuel's work among them they were enjoying a somewhat peaceful period.

In spite of frequent infidelities Yahweh was going forward with His plan to their father Abraham. He, the God of Truth, was keeping His promise. They were no longer wandering tribes. They were a people established in the land of Chanaan. Even now Yahweh was planning to form them into a single prosperous society. He was about to establish them into a kingdom.

When Samuel's age made it necessary to look for a successor, he planned to have his two sons take over his duties. The elders recalled the infidelity of Heli's two sons and would not accept Samuel's plan. The desire to have a king had gained root. Like other nations, they too, wanted a king. Samuel was disturbed. The people of Israel had always been God's own people. Yahweh was their king. He alone made them great and different from all other people. In prayer, Samuel learned God's will. "Samuel," He prompted, "listen to the voice of the people. Give them a king. They have not rejected you but Me."

So, with deep feelings of misgivings, Samuel arranged for a king for Israel. God gave them a king but not the kingship. The king of Israel was merely Yahweh's representative. YAHWEH was their king. Their earthly king would always be subject to Yahweh's prophets.

The change was a great one for Samuel. He did not fear for himself. He was ready and glad to resign. He feared for his people for he knew their weaknesses.

Would they remain faithful to Yahweh? But God's will had been made known and he would carry out the divine command. Samuel wondered who would make the best king for Israel.

Saul

God did not leave Samuel long without explicit direction. "Go about in the countryside of Bethlehem," was the inspired message, "and there meet Saul, son of Cis. He is to be king of Israel. Anoint him."

And so on a road in Bethlehem, Samuel came upon Saul looking about the countryside for his father's donkeys. He was a tall, vigorous man, none finer in all Israel. Saul was astounded at Samuel's message. He could not understand that he had been chosen king, but God had spoken and so it was to be.

During the anointing the Spirit of the Lord came down upon him. The Lord gave Saul a new heart. He went back to his father and his family humbled, and a changed man, but never a word did he say about his strange adventure.

At another message from the Lord, Samuel gathered the elders of all the tribes of Israel at Masphath to cast lots for a king. Tribe by tribe was presented to the Lord. Lot fell upon the tribe of Benjamin. Cis' name was drawn, and the final drawing made Saul king. Saul could not be found. Samuel felt that he must be in hiding, and upon consulting the Lord, he found him in a tent nearby. Samuel prevailed upon him and finally Saul stood before his people, head and shoulders taller than any one of them. Samuel introduced Saul as "The Lord's chosen one." Ringing cheers from every tribe filled the air, "Long live our king."

About four weeks after Israel's king had been acclaimed, the Ammonites threatened the citizens of Jabes-Galaad with fierce cruelty. After a truce of seven days the Ammonites moved toward Jabes-Galaad, and all Saul's forces were at hand. As the Ammonites moved on to make their attack, the Israelites gave them a surprise march from the rear. Destruction was swift; and before the sun had reached its zenith, a great victory had been won. Saul had earned his spurs.

Israel was proud of its king. He had been anointed, accepted, and acclaimed. Now he must be crowned. Samuel called the people to Galgala and here they crowned Saul in the presence of the Lord. Saul was a glad man that day and every man in Israel rejoiced. When the king suggested establishing a place of government in Israel and raising a standing army, all were of one mind with him.

The Philistines watched the Israelites with a careful eye. Saul sent his son Jonathan against a small Philistine garrison. The attack was a success and Saul was encouraged. He sounded an alarm against the Philistines. The enemy mustered all their forces and then the Israelites found themselves hardpressed.

But Saul was a warrior. He was not discouraged. Before his offensive attack, he sent for Samuel to offer a burnt-sacrifice to the Lord. Saul waited and waited but Samuel delayed. Impatient, Saul presumed the privileges of the high priest. He offered the sacrifice. Samuel was indignant at Saul's rashness. Samuel told Saul, "The Lord had destined you to begin a line of kings, but now your dynasty will fall with you." And so it happened.

The battle opened. Resources were all in favor of the Philistines. Their ranks outnumbered the Israelites and they were better equipped. Although Yahweh was displeased with their king, He showed favor toward His people. Under the force of divine power, the ground on which the enemy forces stood shook so that an attack was made impossible. Again the power of Israel's God was shown. The Israelites gave chase to the Philistines.

Saul carried war into the territory of all Israelite enemies in Chanaan. Everywhere he won victories. And then came direction through God's representative, Samuel. Saul received this command, "Destroy Amelec. Spare no one. Take no plunder."

The attack was a success, but Saul spared their king, Agag, and kept the best of their flocks and herds. From that time on Saul was cast off by the Lord. God's spirit passed from him. An evil mood came over him, and he knew no rest. It was hoped that a skillful harpist might relieve the king during these moods. And so it happened that young David, a shepherd boy of Bethlehem, was joined to Saul's court. Saul liked him well.

The Philistines never ceased to give trouble. At one time as the two armies were lined in battle formation on either side of a valley, each day Goliath came forward and challenged any Israelite to fight him single-handed. Now Goliath was a giant, wore a helmet and a breastplate and carried a monstrous spear. Israel was thoroughly discouraged.

Once more David the shepherd boy appeared. Because his brothers had joined Saul's army, David had left the king's court and returned to his father. At this time he had been sent by his father with a message and food for his brothers. David heard Goliath's challenge. Without a sign of fear David said to Saul, "I, my Lord, will battle against this Philistine."

No doubt moved by the Spirit of God, David was deaf to Saul's weak remonstrance. Armed with a shepherd's staff, a sling and five smooth stones in his wallet, the agile shepherd boy sprinted with force toward the great Goliath. Goliath looked at David with scornful contempt. As David ran he adjusted a stone in his sling, aimed, and shot. The shot was expertly done. The small smooth stone imbedded itself deeply into the forehead of his opponent. Goliath fell. David ran, took Goliath's sword and cut off his head. A triumphant cry arose from all Israel. The Philistines betook themselves to flight. Saul insisted that David return to his court.

The wars with the Philistines continued for years. When David grew old enough, his skill as a soldier never failed him. Saul in the end became jealous of David. Twice while the youth was playing the harp in an attempt to soothe the darkness of Saul's mind, Saul tried to take David's life by throwing a lance at him.

Then a new life was forced upon David. He left Saul's court and lived as an outlaw. Saul was determined to kill David and at times during periods of truce with the Philistines, Saul was on David's trail. God protected David. Twice David could have killed Saul but refrained from slaying God's anointed.

And then Saul's final reckoning came. Again the Philistines were at war. Saul and his sons sought safety on Mount Gelboe. Archers followed them and killed Saul's three sons. Saul found refuge in a cave but the archers continued on his trail. Rather than fall alive into the hands of the enemy, Saul fell upon his own sword.

David

1 Samuel 17-30

Although Saul had fallen from his high purpose, the great Lord of Israel did not forget His people. He had chosen the man they needed, one who was brave, tender of heart, and great of mind. Long before Saul's death, the Lord had inspired Samuel to go to the house of Jesse in Bethlehem to anoint David the shepherd boy, the future king of Israel.

Events show that God was always David's strong support. In his youth, all unknowingly, David was being prepared for the great work God wished him to do. His life as shepherd made him gentle toward his flocks and strong against wild, marauding animals. Later as king he was both gentle and valiant. Gifted with musical talent and having the opportunity to play to his heart's content in God's open country, David became an expert harpist and a singer of psalms to God. Eventually his skill on the harp brought him to the royal house of Saul where he learned courtly manners and later secured posts of honor.

The Lord continued directing David's life toward His ends. The bravery David showed in his gallant and successful combat with Goliath never died in the hearts of Israel's warriors. He had saved them. He was their chivalrous hero. And now that there was no king, it was only natural that the elders looked to David. At Hebron he was publicly anointed king of Juda, and there, according to the Lord's counsel, he began his royal work.

Meanwhile, Abner, commander of Saul's army, brought Isboseth, Saul's remaining son, forward and set him up as king of the remaining tribes of Israel. For a long period there was a struggle between Saul's line and David's followers. The conflict went on for seven and a half years, but ever the fortunes and powers of David advanced while the cause of Saul's adherents became ever weaker.

Abner, quietly and discreetly, sent word to David offering him the land and rule of Israel. At the same time he assembled the elders of the tribes and proposed a change. He said to them, "The outcome of this conflict between the two kings of Israel is unmistakable. Let us now go over to David. The time seems at hand when God's prophecy will be fulfilled: 'By David's hands I will rid Israel of the Philistines and all their enemies.' " Abner gained his point without a protest. Faith in the words of God prevailed.

The elders then accompanied Abner to David in Hebron. "We shall rally all Israel to your cause, O King," they said. "We shall be your loyal subjects." The tribes of Jacob were once more united.

David had now to consider a fortress for his citadel. Jerusalem seemed the spot, a place midway between the northern and southern tribes. It belonged to the Jebusites but they candidly told David it would never be his; it was impregnable; it would never fall. But fall it did. Jerusalem, later the glorious stronghold of Israel, was theirs.

A capital city was a great advance for the Israelites, but they were not yet enjoying peace. The Philistine armies waged continual war and besides there were attacks from the Moabites, Ammonites and Syrians. David and his armies were ever at war, but the Lord of hosts was with them. Finally, after years of almost incessant battles, the power of the Philistines was broken and quite naturally the smaller nations made peace also. The promise given to God's Chosen People hundreds of years before, was being fulfilled. Chanaan was their land.

Israel had achieved national unity. David's zeal, however, was not satisfied. The Ark must now be brought to Jerusalem. After many difficulties were surmounted there came a day when all Jerusalem was in joyous spirit. Amid trumpeting, music, and dancing, the Ark, the visible mark of God's presence among them, was brought within the walls of David's city. After it was placed in the midst of the tabernacle prepared for it, burnt-sacrifices and welcome-offerings were made to the Lord. From then on the worship of God was regulated and centered in Jerusalem, God's holy city. Daily sacrifices were offered to Israel's God.

David had lived a just and honorable life but in a moment of weakness he sinned and he sinned seriously. David sinned with the wife of one of his generals, and more than that, he arranged that this general be placed in a precarious position in battle so that he would be killed.

The Lord sent the prophet Nathan to David. Nathan related a story to David about a rich landlord who had flocks and herds in abundance. At one time, wanting to prepare a meal for a guest, the landlord saw fit to rob a poor man of his one pet ewe lamb. David showed great indignation and swore that nothing but death was due this man. Then, Nathan, pointing his finger at David said, "THOU art the man."

David understood. Humbled and sorry for his deed, he said, "I have sinned against the Lord and against my friend."

"The Lord has forgiven thy sin," Nathan gave reply. "Thou shalt not die for it but neither shalt thou be spared punishment."

And so the latter years of David's life were crowded with sufferings. The child born of his unlawful marriage died. Absalom, his favored son, avenged a wrong of his brother Ammon and killed him. Fearing the anger of his father, Absalom lived in exile. After two years, through the influence of friends, Absalom was busy secretly instigating a revolt, and in the end a civil war broke out. David, grieved, left Jerusalem.

After a few days, in the forests of Ephraim, David's armies routed Absalom's followers. As Absalom was fleeing away, riding on the back of a donkey, his long hair caught in the branches of a tree. As he hung there, archers killed him and the civil war came to an end. David grieved over Absalom's death. He wept bitter tears, crying over and over again, "O my son, Absalom, my son, my son. Would I had died instead of you."

These sorrows and others besides were the test of David's repentance, and they gave proof of the greatness of his soul. David impressed the minds of the men of his day as he has those of Christians of all times. His greatness lay in his passionate loyalty to his God and in complete submission to God's will. David as a wise ruler, noble king and loyal servant, faithfully prefigured the eternal kingship of Christ. It was from David's line that Christ was born.

Solomon

David had grown old and lay on his bed, sick. Meanwhile, Adonais, the eldest surviving son, attractive and the general choice, proclaimed, "I will be king."

According to God's plan, however, things were to be otherwise. Years back when Adonais' younger brother was born, God made it known to David through the prophet Nathan that Solomon was the beloved of God and should sit on the throne of his father.

But David was ignorant of what Adonais had done until Bethsabee, the mother of Solomon, and Nathan told him what was going on.

David acted at once. All the important men of state who were not on the usurper's side, were called to David's bedside. "Sit my son Solomon upon my mule," he ordered. "At Gihon let the priests and Nathan anoint him king. Solomon shall sit upon my throne."

After the anointing, amid loud trumpet blasts and much rejoicing, the multitudes cried out, "God save King Solomon." And so, Solomon, according to the Lord's plan, fell heir to the throne of David.

Solomon married the daughter of Pharaoh, king of Egypt. This alliance brought glory and fame to Israel. It linked Israel with one of the great nations of the world, and it eased the tension with the Philistines because Egypt had just won a great victory over them.

Solomon loved the Lord and walked in the precepts of his father David. At Gabaan, one of the high places for sacrifice, Solomon offered a thousand victims as holocausts. The Lord was greatly pleased and appeared to Solomon in a dream at night and said, "Ask what you will and it shall be yours." "Lord," Solomon replied, "give me wisdom that I may rule justly."

The Lord was so pleased with Solomon's request that along with wisdom the Lord promised him riches and glory. Solomon's wealth was fabulous. Even to this day he is known as the wisest and richest man that ever lived. No court has seen the glory, splendor and renown of Solomon's.

In all cases Solomon's decisions were most just. Once two women pleaded their quarrel. One woman had a dead baby in her arms. The other woman's baby was alive. The first claimed that the woman with the live baby took her live baby from her while she was asleep and put her own dead baby in its place. The woman with the live baby said the story was untrue and that the live child she held in her arms was her own child.

After hearing both women, Solomon called a soldier to him and ordered him to take the live infant, cut it in half, and give half to each mother. The woman who claimed that her child was alive, dropped to her knees and offered the child to Solomon saying, "Sir, spare my child's life. I will gladly give it up alive to this woman who wrongly claims it."

Solomon solved the problem. He knew now who was mother to the child. He said to the kneeling woman, "Keep the child. It is yours." All Israel heard the judgment. They feared their king, seeing that the wisdom of God was in him.

The Israelites were gaining distinction among the nations. They had a king who was living at peace with their neighbors; wealth was pouring into their country. Besides, their ruler had a master-mind. He knew the secrets of nature. He could tell about the growth of every kind of tree and plant. He knew the ways of animals, birds, and fishes. He knew these and other things of nature, not through learning, but by the special gift God had given him. Solomon was pleasing to God.

And now the Lord chose Solomon to do a singular work for Him. Solomon was to build a temple to the Lord. He did it well, with great joy and fervor. It was seven years in building and thousands were employed. The very finest materials were brought from distant lands. Rare cedar wood was brought from Lebanon and marble and granite blocks were quarried for its walls. The whole interior was lined with plates of the purest gold. Altar vessels were made of gold and silver and ornamented with many-colored jewels. Tapestries, of pleasing colors and design, were supported by tall, bronze columns. Everywhere there were riches and beauty to give honor and glory to God.

Then followed the glorious dedication of this great temple to the most high God. King Solomon sent a summons to the elders, and to all the people to come to Jerusalem to assist at the moving of the Ark from the City of Sion where it had been resting. The priests and the Levites took up the Ark and the Tabernacle, and King Solomon walked before it and with him a great throng of Israelites.

After the Ark was set in its new and permanent place, the Holy of Holies, victims of sheep and oxen were sacrificed. Suddenly the whole interior of the temple was wreathed in a thick cloud. God's own glory came down visibly in the form of a cloud and filled His own house. Solomon, standing at the altar, lifted his arms to heaven. In a loud voice, in a long and fervent prayer, he praised God. When he had finished, he knelt on the ground in great reverence and then stood and turned to bless his people.

Thousands of burnt-sacrifices and welcome-offerings were made. There were so many that no account was taken of them. The ceremony lasted fourteen days after which the king and all the people returned to their homes thanking God for His mercy and His blessings.

One of the saddest happenings in human history is that Solomon did not remain true to the God Who had been so faithful to him. After years of devoted service, Solomon showed a changed mind toward God. God tried to prevent his fall. He appeared to him praising him for his faithfulness and then giving this warning, "Hold true to My observance and to My decrees. If you and your children turn to false gods, Israel shall fall and the Temple you have erected will be thrust out of My sight."

But Solomon did not heed God's warning. Pride in his kingdom and love for pagan women had entered his soul. He was busy building quarters for his horsemen and their chariots. He was busy in fortifying Israel's unexcelled cities and in building more cities. But what gave the greatest offense to God was that he built temples to the false gods of his pagan wives, and to please them, even worshiped in them. As God's blessing was withdrawn from Solomon, the unity of Israel broke down. The spirit of God's Chosen People crumbled until only a remnant remained. Once more through sin God's plan to spread His kingdom had to be changed.

127

The Division of the Kingdom

UNIT VIII
GOD'S JUDGMENT FALLS ON ISRAEL

The stories of Unit VIII are taken from the Books of Kings, Tobit, Judith, Esther, Job, Isaiah, Jeremiah, Ezechiel, Daniel and Jonah.

After Solomon's death, disputes arose and Israel was divided into the Kingdom of Juda and the Kingdom of Israel. Unrest and quarreling followed.

Sin continued but God remained faithful. Punish His people He must and as always, in repentance many again returned to Him.

During this trying period the voice of God's prophets and the influence of strong men and women kept the realization of God's love and mercy ever before the minds of this people, so unworthy of love and yet so strongly loved by God.

THE DIVISION OF THE KINGDOM

1 Kings 12

Upon Solomon's death his kingdom was divided. Roboam, his son, went to Sichem where all Israel was assembled to crown him king. They made a request to Roboam. "Your father," they said, "made us bear a bitter yoke. Do you show clemency and we will be your loyal servants."

In reply Roboam said, "If my father's yoke fell heavily upon you, mine will be heavier still." When the people realized Roboam's attitude, they were quick with their answer. "David's line is not for us," they cried.

All the Jews of the northern tribes went to their homes and formed the Northern Kingdom. Jeroboam, who had been out of favor with Solomon, was acclaimed their king. This schism cut the Northern Kingdom off from the succession to the royal line of David.

Only the tribe of Juda and the small tribe of Benjamin, a mere remnant of the Jewish nation, remained the Chosen People of God. Jerusalem, the Holy City, continued to be their capital and Roboam their king.

Jeroboam, fearing that the hearts of his people would think longingly of their great temple at Jerusalem, apostatized. He built rival sanctuaries at Bethel and Dan where the Lord was worshiped under the form of a bull. There was no blessing on the land. Jeroboam and all who reigned after him were continually besieged by foreign peoples. Finally, Israel, the Northern Kingdom, made an unfortunate alliance with Syria. After a short time Syria and Israel with it, fell into the hands of the Assyrians, then masters of the north country. Judaism in Israel was at an end.

Juda was not cast off from the Lord as was Israel. Its future was to be glorious because it carried within it the seed of the royal line of David. Its present condition, however, was one of debasement. During repeated wars the glorious temple at Jerusalem was reduced to ruins, and finally, the proud city became a puppet state to Babylon.

Now when Nabuchodonosor became emperor of Babylon, he was determined to put an end to the national spirit of the Jews. He sent thousands into exile. Those that were sent to Egypt were lost to Egyptian manners and customs.

The exiles in Babylon under the influence of the God-sent prophets, Daniel and Ezechiel, persevered in their religious practices. At the end of the captivity, they returned to Juda with a burning zeal to renew their loyalty to the one true God and to rebuild His Holy City, Jerusalem.

TOBIAS

Tobit

Tobias was a God-fearing man who was exiled to Ninive. The exiled Jews were made to suffer, and Tobias used his time and riches to give his country-men food and clothing. He cared for the sick and buried the dead.

One night, weary and tired, he lay under a tree. The dung from a nest fell on his eyes, blinding him. In all his trials Tobias saw God's justice and love.

Financial difficulties came and Tobias remembered a loan he had made Gabelus of Rages in Media. "Son," he said to young Tobias, "find a man of some credit as companion and go to Gabelus and redeem the loan I made to him."

As Tobias left the house on his errand, a well-dressed man approached him and offered his service as guide. In an interview both father and son were completely convinced that this unknown person was trust-worthy. Strangely, too, he seemed to foreknow the errand and even the persons and places concerned. He did know. He was the angel Raphael but introduced himself as Azarius. In all experiences along the road Azarius was ever right and ready in his decision. He saved Tobias from the fierce attack of a monstrous fish. "Preserve the gall, heart and liver," he ordered.

131

Tobias

Later, when they neared the home of Tobias' kinsman, Raguel, Azarius suggested that Tobias ask for the hand of Sarah. Tobias agreed. Without hesitation, he put his fears aside. Fears might well have stopped him. Sarah had already married seven times and each time death came to the bridegroom. But not now. The marriage was happily performed and joy followed.

During the marriage feast, Azarius offered to go to Gabelus to collect the money due Tobias, and on his return plans were made for a happy homeward trip.

The travelers were sighted in the distance and soon there was ready a warm welcome from family and friends. By direction from Azarius, Tobias anointed his father's eyes with the gall of the fish. His sight returned.

Tobias' home abounded in joy; sight returned, a son safe home with a beautiful wife, and money to ease the days of want. God was good!

As Tobias offered recompense to Azarius, Azarius explained, "I am the Angel Raphael." The household was amazed. They were filled with awe and terror. "Do not be afraid," said Raphael. Peace came. And as they yet knelt, Raphael disappeared from their midst.

The Book of Tobias is still considered a story of historic facts. The Church has as yet not given definite decision to any contrary opinion and yet we should allow for such who interpret it as historic fiction unless the Church should decide against such a belief. Be this as it may, the account, like all Biblical stories has a definite lesson God wishes us to think about. In this instance we are impressed with the edifying life of a pious Israelite observing the Law of Moses far away from his homeland, living among pagans. In both posterity and misfortune, Tobias and his son give us a worthy example of perfect resignation.

Judith

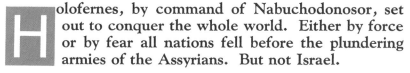oloffernes, by command of Nabuchodonosor, set out to conquer the whole world. Either by force or by fear all nations fell before the plundering armies of the Assyrians. But not Israel.

Eliachim, the high priest, asked that the invading forces be resisted. Jerusalem and the sacred Temple were not to be desecrated.

Bethulia was built on a rocky pass and offered a direct entrance into Juda. Holofernes knew it was easy to maintain and hard to attack. He considered. "There will be no battle," he said. "Cut off the city's water supply."

Within days the Bethulites were suffering. But their elders encouraged trust in God. After twenty days the whole populace pleaded that surrender be made. Ozias addressed his suffering subjects, "Continue in prayer. If within five days relief does not come, we will surrender."

Judith, a chaste and noble widow, was inspired by God to save her people. Without revealing her plan, but with the consent and prayers of the elders, she set about her strategy.

By night Judith and her maid left the gates of Bethulia and at early dawn reached the Assyrian camp. Beautifully attired and pretending to have deserted her people, Judith won favor with Holofernes. Her requests were graciously granted. She and her maid were to live in the camp unmolested. They were free to come and go as they would. Each night they left camp to perform a washing of religious rite and to pray.

On the fourth day of Judith's stay in camp, Holofernes felt flattered when Judith accepted an invitation to dine with him and his generals. Holofernes and his men knew no restraint. One by one the generals left, each just about able to depart. Holofernes lay in his tent in a drunken stupor.

This was brave Judith's moment. She acted quickly. With Holofernes' own sword she cut off his head, and once more and for the last time, she and her maid walked

Esther

unmolested through the camp, past the sentry. Little did the sentry dream that their leather bag held the gory head of Assyria's general. Judith and her maid walked on to Bethulia.

At Judith's call the gates of the city were opened wide. Strangely, fear had gone. By dawn, Israel's forces took to arms with great shouts and trumpet blasts. The Assyrian army fled, fearing to face people whose God 'marshals the armies of heaven.' Jerusalem and God's Temple were saved from assault.

The story of Judith is history mixed with fiction. From the beginning the Church has considered this book of the Bible as divinely inspired. The author portrays Judith in a daring adventure to save God's people from an imminent disaster. Judith shows unusual courage, she is motivated by high ideals and acts with a spirit of heroic patriotism. Faced with a similar calamity, the story of this inspired writer encourages the people of his time to have absolute confidence in God.

ESTHER

Esther

Assuerus was king of Persia in which lived many devout Jews. Among these was Mardocai whose brother had died and left to his care an only child, a daughter, Esther. Mardocai adopted her as his daughter and brought her up to know a father's love.

Assuerus felt he had to have a new queen. Vasthi, his royal wife, had refused to obey his command. The kingdom was searched to find a queen, a woman of beauty and loveliness. Many fair and noble ladies were considered. Of them all, Esther, to her father's great delight, became queen. Esther, at Mardocai's prudent admonition, never identified herself as a Jewess.

It was at this time that high courtly favor, a place next to the king, was given to Aman. While others paid honor to Aman, Mardocai did not. This slight bothered Aman very much. Later when Aman learned that Mardocai was a Jew, he spitefully planned a plot against his people. Aman requested Assuerus to sign an edict he had prepared which demanded the massacre of every Jew in the realm. Assuerus signed it. After-events showed, however, that the king very likely had not even read the document.

The Jews donned sackcloth and ashes. Mardocai, with great dispatch, got word to Queen Esther to speak to the king for her people. Discreetly Esther made her plans. Three days were spent in prayer and without food or drink. At the risk of her own life, she planned to enter the audience chamber of the king to invite Assuerus and Aman to a banquet where she would tell what troubled her. All plans succeeded admirably except that even at the king's urging, Esther was unable to divulge her trouble. She promised though that on the next day, at a second banquet with the same guests, she would tell her trouble.

The next day, bravely and without a trace of fear, Esther pleaded the cause of her people who had always been faithful subjects. Once Assuerus understood the terrible plight of the Jews, he was moved. "Who," he asked, "has drawn up this cruel edict?" Esther pointed to Aman who had become silent and fearful.

Conditions reversed rapidly. Aman was hung on a gibbet he had erected for Mardocai. Jews all through the country were held in higher esteem and in many cases were moved into important positions. Mardocai was made the king's first minister.

The Book of Esther is an historical story of a modest and simple Jewish maiden struggling for her people against the revenge and intrigue of a powerful enemy. These rivals play their roles in the splendor of a Persian court. Based on history as it is, the story is enhanced with poetic beauty and is linked with religion.

As we study Biblical stories we become more and more familiar with God's plan in favor of His Chosen People to raise up inspired and prophetic writers who portray through their writings a moral and religious influence. This story was written to put heart into a nation that needed to exercise heroic trust in Divine Providence.

lthough Job was not a Jew, he was a God-fearing man. He was rich and blessed with sons and daughters and enjoyed an excellent reputation.

Satan in an interview with God said that there was much wickedness on earth and that he met with little opposition. God asked if he had considered His servant Job. The devil replied, "Your servant Job has no cause to rebel. Let suffering come to him and then he will blaspheme You just as others do." God accepted Satan's challenge.

Satan planned to strip Job of all the things he possessed. With brutal swiftness, heartbreaking messages were brought to Job. While his children were feasting, a tempestuous wind wrecked the house and all were killed. Bands of robbers swept down on his oxen and asses and drove them away through the mountain passes. Lightning killed all his sheep and shepherds. In three groups Chaldeans stole his camels and killed the men in charge.

Through all these calamities Job uttered no word against God. He bowed his head in submission saying, "The Lord has given and the Lord has taken away. Blessed be the name of the Lord."

Satan went back to God and admitted his surprise. He said, "Job did indeed accept his losses well, but touch his person; then he will blaspheme."

Again, with God's consent, Job was put to a further test. From the crown of his head to the soles of his feet, Job's body was afflicted with sores. His wife was no comfort to him and neither were his intimate friends, Elphaz, Baldad and Sophas. They added to his misery. They insisted that Job had grievously sinned and only by repentance, they repeatedly told him, would God show mercy. Job wearied telling them again and again that he was innocent. Finally, his would-be comforters spoke no more.

After months of physical suffering, poverty and loneliness, suddenly, from the midst of a whirlwind, the Lord

Job

gave Job comfort. By questions God opened Job's mind. "Job, do you understand all about the stars, the wind, the clouds, the rain? I direct them all. Do you know the habits and the haunts of all animals? I know their strength and give them their food. These and many other things cannot be explained and you will never understand them." And then with great kindness and understanding the Lord added, "Neither can suffering be explained. I measure it and know when and where to send it. Always trust Me."

Job, consoled, bowed in humble understanding and answered the Lord, "I am of little account; what can I answer You?"

A new spirit came over Job. He raised another family, made many friends and recovered more riches than he had before Satan tried him. His latter days were richly blessed and he died, old and full of years.

Job is an historical figure and the record of his life as given in the Bible was written under inspiration to teach us an important lesson. Job shows us how to suffer patiently, without resentment and even joyously. Thoughts of Job's patience will help us in our suffering if in spirit we can say with him, "The Lord has given and the Lord has taken away; blessed be the name of the Lord."

Elias

Achab, king of Israel, had defied the Lord and had done wickedly. His marriage to Jezabel made his condition even worse. God's temples were destroyed and altars were built to the god Baal.

Elias, prophet of the Most High, moved by the spirit, sought the presence of the king unannounced. Fearlessly he foretold God's punishment. A drought would come upon Samaria and all the adjacent land. And so it happened. All living things suffered.

Immediately thereupon, word from the Lord came to Elias to move eastward to a stream. There, morning and evening, a raven supplied him with food. Elias remained there until the river became parched.

The Lord did not forsake His servant. "Leave this place," He said. Going to the town of Serepta he met a widow in the act of gathering faggots to prepare a last meal for her son and herself. Elias was made welcome, and from that day until the rain fell again, the widow's flour and oil never gave out.

When two years had gone by, the Lord God told Elias to confront Achab. Elias came upon the king in the open country. Elias told Achab to send out couriers to announce a gathering of all Israel on Mount Carmel. Proof would be made before the whole populace whether the God of Israel or Baal was the one true God.

On the mountain top the four hundred and fifty prophets of Baal assembled to contend against Elias. Two altars of stone were erected. Wood was put in place and the slaughtered bulls were laid upon them. No fire was to be applied to either sacrifice. At the prayers of the respective prophets fire was to be enkindled miraculously to consume the holocaust. Neither time, prayer nor the frenzied antics of Baal's prophets were effective. But, immediately at the fervent prayer of Elias, a divine fire fell, consuming victim, wood, and even the altar built of stone. The people fell face to earth and cried, "The Lord is God. He is the almighty and everlasting God." When Elias completed his work on earth, he was carried away in a flaming chariot drawn by flaming horses. In a whirlwind Elias was taken into heaven. His mantle fell upon his disciple Eliseus who was to succeed him as prophet in Israel.

Isaias

Isaias, one of the greatest of all prophets, was born of a distinguished family in Jerusalem about eight centuries before Christ.

Isaias was a devout man and frequented the sacred temple. During one of his visits he had a vision. He saw the Lord in wondrous glory sitting on a throne. Six-winged Seraphim moved in splendor about Him and ever the same cry passed among them, "Holy, holy,holy is the Lord God of hosts, all the earth is full of His glory." All space rang with the sound of that cry and smoke went up, filling the Temple courts.

Isaias, kneeling and listening to the holy cry, regretted that his lips had sinned. He was not worthy to pronounce these blessed words. Whereupon a Seraphim flew to him with a burning coal and touched his lips and said, "Now your guilt is swept away. Your sin is pardoned."

The Lord then said, "Who shall be My messenger?"

Isaias answered, "I am here at Your command; make me Your messenger." With this, Isaias was ordained God's prophet.

At this time Juda was at the height of her prosperity, but wealth and relations with foreign nations weakened her spirit. Juda needed a messenger from God. For almost fifty years Isaias preached to God's people of repentance and penance. He preached against idolatry; he threatened the rich and the powerful; he condemned the sensual. He urged all to repentance and faith.

Without fear he warned ruling powers of their selfish, foreign connections. When the policy of the prophet's advice to rely on God alone for the safety of Juda clashed against that of authority and an alliance was drawn up with Assyria, Isaias knew the exile was about to take place. Only a remnant of God's people, the best of their offspring would return to build a new Jerusalem.

When devastation lay heavily upon his people and the nation was being exploited, Isaias raised their hopes. He preached with great fervor about the holy Seed, meaning Christ the Savior Who was to come and save Israel from complete destruction. He prophesied the coming of the Messias.

Jeremias

Jeremiah

Jeremias was a Benjamite born of a family of priests. He was brought up with a high esteem for God and the Law of God. When still a young man the word of the Lord came, telling Jeremias to give a prophet's message to the nation.

Now Jeremias may have been slow of speech or at least he felt timid about accepting so great a task. He said, "I am but a child."

"Have no human fears," came the reply. "Am I not at your side to protect you?" And with that the Lord touched Jeremias on the mouth.

"See," He said, "I have inspired your lips with speech. I give you authority over nations and over kingdoms everywhere."

Jeremias warned the people of the fall of Jerusalem. Often when he gave his doleful message that the temple would be destroyed, that the wealth of their city would be the spoil of Babylon, the populace laughed him to scorn. Once he was beaten and put into stocks. Another time he was lowered into a cistern of mire but a slave freed him.

From time to time Jeremias complained to the Lord, but after He had comforted him God always gave him another message of woe to foretell. And then with still greater zeal Jeremias tried to bring his own people, the Chosen People, to sorrow and repentance.

But civic affairs were shaping to a climax. King Josias opposed the Egyptian army but was soon overcome. Warfare continued until Nabuchodonosor himself entered Jerusalem.

Later, King Sedecius made an alliance with Egypt and several neighboring kings against Nabuchodonosor. And then the woeful prophecies of Jeremias found fulfillment. Babylon besieged Jerusalem. After eighteen months of bitter suffering for the Jews, a breach was made in the great walls of the Holy City. The poor were massacred and the wealthy taken into captivity to Babylon.

Jeremias' life of preaching was over. He dwelt amid the ruins of the temple until he was kidnapped by rebellious Jews and taken to Egypt where he finally died.

Ezechiel

Ezechiel

During the seventy years of the Babylonian Captivity, the Israelites were not treated as captives but rather as exiles. They enjoyed considerable freedom, and were given land to cultivate. Trades and crafts were established.

Success in the externals of life did not relieve the deep hurt of the spirit. Homesickness filled the heart. The beautiful Temple was theirs no more. Having no temple, they had no sacrifice. The unrestrained life of the Babylonians and the cult of pagan practices opened temptation to them and to their children. Israel was living through darkness and despair.

Their sufferings were of their own making. As did their forebears, so they, too, had rebelled against a provident God Who had repeatedly performed great wonders to make them a nation at all. And of all nations, He made them His chosen race. This period of exile was a time of mercy and purification.

Ezechiel, a young man who was in exile, being alone one day in the open country, suddenly saw God in a vision of glory. Seeing God's splendor, Ezechiel fell down, face to earth. At the voice and command of God a divine force brought Ezechiel to his feet. God's voice said, "Son of man, I am sending you to the remnant of a rebellious people. Reprove them. All the words I tell you, heed and hear. Give your message in the name of the Lord God." Ezechiel tells that the message being finished, there was a great noise behind him and the vision was gone.

Ezechiel preached God's anger against His people with earnestness and zeal. His hearers were not impressed. False prophets preached a happier message and the shrines of the false gods continued to lure God's chosen ones to a pagan world. But Ezechiel never wearied. He knew how grave was his responsibility. When he told his people that Jerusalem was about to fall, they believed otherwise. Such disaster could never happen to Jerusalem. But, the blow came and with it the hearts of the people changed. Ezechiel, to give to his people

149

Daniel

encouragement, preached to them of a new Jerusalem. Hope and repentance purified their souls. When the captivity was over, exiled Israel returned a humbled people, ready to follow the guidance of the Lord.

DANIEL
Daniel

Nabuchodonosor, during the siege at Jerusalem, called his head chamberlain and entrusted to him the care and education of four young Israelites of royal stock, comely in appearance and keen of mind. They were Daniel, Ananias, Misael, and Azarias.

These young men were to be put on probation for three years and after that time they were to be presented to Nabuchodonosor himself. The period of probation was given to studies which included the lore and language of the Chaldeans. Of the four, Daniel was especially gifted.

Their probation completed, the chamberlain presented his charges to the king who was greatly pleased with the advancement his new subjects had made. In all the kingdom there was no match to be found for them. Never a question but they could answer it with quick wit.

Daniel, by his wisdom and popularity, became the most honored member of the royal suite. God gifted him particularly with the power to tell the meaning of dreams. Among pagans this power was important because dreams, especially dreams of kings, were supposed to forbode events that were to come. Every kingdom had its schools of diviners, sages and soothsayers. Daniel was never classified as one of these, but when these failed to interpret a dream, Daniel was called on. His interpretation came through divine assistance and never failed.

At one time Daniel was responsible for destroying one of the heathen gods and its priests were massacred. The people were in a rage and demanded that Daniel be given up. They threw him into a den among lions. The lions did not hurt him and on the seventh day the king had him released.

Daniel was a man of action. He rebuked kings and exposed frauds, especially those regarding false reli-

Jonas

gions. He worked and prayed for his own people, many of whom had gone astray. Some were very indifferent and languid and there were those, too, who were resentful at being Israelites at all. He was a prophet who raised the hopes of the people in a new and glorious Jerusalem, and above all in the coming of the Messias.

Daniel did not return to the land of his birth.

JONAS

Jonah

Ninive was an ancient pagan city and so wicked, the vengeance of God was about to destroy it. Then the voice of God came to Jonas the prophet, "Make your way to Ninive. I would have you preach to them. Warn them that I have knowledge of their guilt."

At the command, Jonas arose but not to obey. His plan was to get out of the way of the Lord. At Joppa he boarded a ship bound for Tharsis. Instead of moving east toward Ninive he planned to sail west as far as he could go.

The boat was scarcely on its way when a destructive wind blew over the sea, threatening shipwreck. Jonas was extremely tired because of his hurried walk to get to the boat and already lay in the ship's hold in a deep sleep. The captain finding him so, shouted, "Man, wake up. We are perishing. Call upon your God for help."

The storm continued to rage until the sailors finally suggested casting lots to find out who among them was responsible for this sudden storm. The lot fell upon Jonas. Stunned and contrite now, Jonas acknowledged his disobedience to the will of God. He knew that God's anger was against him and had caused the storm. To save the lives of the others, Jonas suggested that they throw him overboard. The sailors did so and immediately there was a change. The force of the wind lessened and a gentle breeze helped the ship on its way.

At the Lord's bidding a great seabeast swallowed Jonas. There in the belly of the beast Jonas promised obedience if the Lord would spare him. After three days the seabeast cast Jonas on dry land.

153

This time Jonas lost no time finding Ninive. Throughout the streets of the great city Jonas cried out the Lord's message, "In forty days Ninive will be destroyed."

Hearing this, the Ninivites from the king down showed faith in God. A fast was proclaimed for both man and beast. The king's message was at once proclaimed throughout the kingdom, "Let us pray and do penance. God may relent and pardon us." God heard their prayer and accepted their penance and Ninive was spared.

Jonas was exceedingly troubled and angry at the turn of events. As he had been told, he had preached God's vengeance and now mercy was shown. God had patience with Jonas. He knew that he was human. For comfort God provided the shade of an ivy plant, under which the prophet sat sulking in the eastern section of the city. Jonas was exceedingly glad of the ivy. But in God's plan, by morning a worm struck the ivy and it withered. The sun beat down on Jonas. He cried out, "It is better for me to die than to live."

And then the Lord said to Jonas, "Do you think you have any reason to be angry over the ivy? You did not plant it; it cost you no toil. It is merely a plant that springs up in a night and in another it withers. And what of Ninive? Here is a great city with a hundred and twenty thousand persons in it, and none of them can tell right from left, all these cattle too; and may I not spare Ninive?"

Many Catholics consider this story as genuine history. But in the opinion of numerous critics who follow the view of Saint Gregory of Nazianzen, it is not historic. It is a fictitious story aimed to teach a spiritual lesson which was much needed at that time. It is considered one of the greatest of the parables given in the Old Testament.

It was written, no doubt, by a priest who understood much better than did the Jews of his day, the great mercy of God. It aims also to show that while the Jews had the honor of being the nation selected by God for His special revelation, He did not want them to narrow their religion to their own people only. God wanted them to spread the knowledge of His power, mercy and love to other nations. Israel must be His missionary. The story likewise prepared the Israelites themselves to accept the world redeeming character of God's plan to save all men. The time of Christ was drawing near.

UNIT IX
ISRAEL AGAIN FINDS FAVOR WITH GOD

The stories of Unit IX are taken from the Book of Aggeus, the Book of Zachariah, the first Book of Esdras, the Book of Nehemiah, the Book of Malachias, the first Book of Machabees and the second Book of Machabees.

Because of its persistent practice of idolatry, the Kingdom of Israel was destroyed and its people dispersed among other nations.

Juda alternated between sin and repentance. Finally God permitted its people to be overcome, and they were sent into exile.

The history of the Jewish people continues with these exiles who were forced to go to Babylon.

Here God sent prophets with messages of comfort and hope. Through suffering, these exiles finally repented and sincerely returned to God.

During the reign of King Cyrus, this remnant of the Jewish race was finally allowed to return to Jerusalem and rebuild the temple.

Return of the Exiles

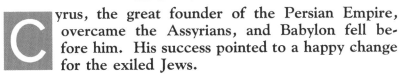
Ezra 1-3

Cyrus, the great founder of the Persian Empire, overcame the Assyrians, and Babylon fell before him. His success pointed to a happy change for the exiled Jews.

Cyrus respected the religion of his subjects and proposed that the Jews return to their native land, which now was a Persian province. He urged them to rebuild their sacred temple, and he restored to them the sacred vessels which had been plundered by the Babylonians.

In the spring of 537 B. C., Cyrus appointed Zorobabel governor of Judea and Joshua its high priest. More than forty-two thousand Jews with all their possessions moved from Babylon to Judea.

The Jews of the Babylonian Captivity were of the wealthier class and were better educated than most of their brethren. During the years of captivity they had developed a new religious fervor. The generations that followed did not lack the high ideals of their elders, and on returning to Jerusalem, they began with great zeal to improve their city and to rebuild their glorious Temple.

It took six months to re-establish themselves. Clans and families sought their own homes. Ruined houses were rebuilt and inhabited ones were purchased from the occupants. Many settled in temporary shelters and tents.

During the seventh month of their return, rebuilding the temple was begun. While they had been in exile in Babylon, the prophet Ezechiel had filled the hearts of this remnant of the Chosen People with an ardent desire to restore Yahweh's sacrificial altar. He emphasized it as their duty because only through this purified remnant could Judaism be restored. Now that they had the opportunity to accomplish their desire, they faced their problem with courage and determination. Soon an altar, on which sacrifices could be offered, was erected. After this they began to work on the foundation of the temple for which they had already collected building materials, even cedars from Lebanon. But quickly bitter opposition confronted them.

157

Aggeus and Zacharias

The forefathers of these exiled Jews had suffered God's severe chastisement because of their intimate relations with other peoples. Hence these fervent Jews returning to the land of their fathers to rebuild their race and their religion, were not going to repeat this error. They would have no social dealings with foreign nations nor even with those of their own race who through marriage were contaminated with other gods. Naturally this exclusive attitude aroused opposition, especially from the Samaritans who became their bitterest enemies.

By intrigue with local officials, the Samaritans and others managed to block plans for restoring religious worship to Yahweh exclusively. The Samaritans would have been willing to assist in the building of the temple to Yahweh, but not to Yahweh alone, for they believed in worshiping other gods as well.

As a result of this opposition and also through lack of resources and workers, the exiles finally gave up the idea of restoring the temple. Other problems presented themselves and for fifteen years they worked to improve their material condition. They had to resume the building and conditioning of houses. Moreover, to save their families from want, they had to clear and prepare the soil for agriculture. During this period their religious enthusiasm weakened. Later, though, Yahweh raised up prophets to revive it, but the struggle was not won until almost a hundred years later.

AGGEUS AND ZACHARIAS
Ezra 4

The exiles had now been living in Judea for sixteen years. During these years their families had become well-housed and profitably established in business and agriculture, but there were still many more advances to be made.

They were neighbors to people with whom there could be no friendly relations. These resented the ambitions of the exiles to advance Jerusalem into a powerful and prosperous state. The matter of religion was ever a drawback. The plan to rebuild the temple and re-establish sacrificial practices on Mount Sion was particularly offensive to the Jews not of the Babylonian Captivity. These had intermarried with the Samaritans and foreign neighbors and dreaded the enforcement of strict observance of the Law of Moses. The returned exiles, on the other hand, persevered in their earnestness about a reformed religious life. Their exclusiveness on law and religion was a reproach to their fallen brethren. There was constant friction to be overcome.

Discouragement lowered the ardor of these fervent Jews. Their efforts slackened. Even Zorobabel and Joshua no longer urged them to rebuild their Temple.

And then God intervened. About 520 B.C. a message came from the Lord through His prophet Aggeus to Zorobabel, the governor, to Joshua, the highpriest, and to all the people, "Do you say it is too early to restore My temple? You have roofs over your heads. Now make a shelter for your God. Go to the hillside and fetch timber."

Zorobabel and Joshua and all the people could not but heed the voice of the Lord God given them through Aggeus. Aggeus gave not only a command to God's Chosen Ones, but also words of divine encouragement. They received the Lord's own assurance that He was on their side. And the Lord put heart into them, governor, priest, and people alike.

Zacharias was another prophet of this time. He was a younger man than Aggeus and his message quite different. Aggeus directed the people to an understanding of man's redemption. Zacharias' aim was for a change of heart. He was directing his hearers to a right attitude of mind toward truth and mercy. Zacharias anticipated the teaching of the New Testament. The drift of his teaching can be likened to the spirit of the Beatitudes. As the time for Christ's appearance neared, the teachings of the Old Testament portrayed ever more and more the spirit of the Redeemer Himself.

The groundwork for rebuilding Jerusalem had a fair beginning, but the obstacles hindering the plans of those who had been courageous enough to return to the land of their fathers, were greater than so small a group could overcome. Artaxerxes, the Persian king of Babylon, followed the example of Cyrus. He was instrumental in sending a zealous priest named Esdras to lead another large group of Jewish exiles back to Palestine.

Esdras, priest and scribe, had great influence. He carried with him letters from the king authorizing him to undertake the leadership and to direct the religious life of the community.

During the years of captivity in Babylon the Jews missed their sacred temple and felt lost because they had no place to worship. The idea of a synagogue, a meeting place, the center of their religious life developed at this period. In these assemblies in the synagogues on the Sabbath and feast days, a program of prayer, singing of psalms, and reading from the Scrolls, the Books of the Law, was followed. Esdras was chiefly responsible for this mode of religious service. His enthusiastic interest in the Books of the Law, the five Books of Moses, exerted a new influence on the lives of the people.

So, it truly seemed that Yahweh, through the Persian rulers, directed affairs in favor of His beloved Chosen People. Soon synagogues were erected in their newly found home, and a revived interest in the Law was strongly maintained. Esdras aimed at strict observance and was inflexible when there was a question of marriage with a non-Israelite. He dissolved all marriages with foreign wives.

Esdras moved the hearts of the people profoundly, but there was need in Jerusalem for more than a change of heart. The city needed unification. It needed a ruler. For this work the Lord singled out Nehemias, a strong, persistent man who was in great favor at the king's court in Babylon.

Esdras and Nehemias

Previous to the coming of Nehemias, attempts had been made to build a wall around Jerusalem, but it was never achieved. Jerusalem was still an open city, exposed to the attacks of hostile neighbors. Nehemias acted cautiously. He concealed his project and during three nights secretly made a thorough study of the condition of what remained of the city walls. He then revealed his position among them and his plan. The people were overjoyed to have a leader and considered his plan to complete the walls about Jerusalem, excellent. The builders divided into parties and worked rapidly. Within a short time the walls and one well were completed. It was a great triumph. However, again the opposition party, the Samaritans, made trouble. Indeed, Nehemias had his enemies; he was all but assassinated.

But with time and much struggle Jerusalem became a strong citadel. These persevering Judeans accomplished much. They were the illustrious remnant from which developed a new and glorious Israel, the Israel from which the Redeemer would arise. To be so distinguished, had always been the boast and dream of all true Israelites.

Malachias

Malachy

After the return from Babylon the hearts of the favored ones of God's Chosen People were full of fervor. The temple had been restored and sacrifice was again being offered to God. Throughout the land synagogues had been erected and the Sabbath was being properly observed.

But after years of well-doing, the preachings of the prophets were forgotten and evil had its way once more. Both priests and people were guilty. Sin found its way to the very altar of God. The priests dared to offer unworthy sacrifices to the all Holy One. The people neglected to pay temple tithes and, worse still, mixed marriages and divorces were common.

God's favor was withdrawn and Judea was suffering misery. The great hope to become an independent people faded. They were still under Persian domination. Now drought ruined their crops and locusts devastated their land.

Had their faith been strong, they would have recognized God's punishments as marks of His love to draw them to Himself. But instead they blamed God. They questioned His love for them as a nation.

God had not forsaken them. To bring His people to repentance God sent His prophet Malachias. Malachias was the last of the long line of prophets before John the Baptist. As in the case of all other prophets, Malachias, too, had a particular message from God.

Malachias spoke strongly to his hearers. He made them understand Yahweh's love for them and their sorry return of that love. He told of Yahweh's weariness at their indifference and His hurt at the sinfulness of their priests. The thought of God's mercy, though, was not wanting in the preaching of Malachias. He encouraged his hearers to repent because only then would they again experience the effects of divine goodness. "God's coming," he said, "would be as fire to destroy all wickedness and also to refine the good in them."

Machabees

uring four hundred years Judea was ruled by various powers. Except for heavy taxation and now and then some minor troubles, the country was left in peace.

Then, about the year 176 B.C., Antiochus, a Syrian, governed the land. His reign brought misery and suffering. Seemingly, his rule, according to God's plan, was a final purification of the remnant of God's Chosen People. Through persecutions and wars the vigor of many souls was revealed.

At first, Antiochus introduced a pagan Greek spirit into the life of Israel. It was not accepted. One day, on entering Jerusalem in great military pomp, he went into the holy temple and even into the Holy of Holies and robbed it of its treasures. All Judea was shocked. Two years later a statue of Jupiter was placed on the altar of sacrifice in the temple, and a decree went out that the citizens were to partake of the flesh meat which had been offered to the pagan gods. Refusal meant death.

A bloody persecution followed. Mothers endured shame and death for having their sons circumcised. A large group who had assembled to celebrate the Sabbath were burnt alive. Eleazar, one of the chief scribes, was savagely beaten to death. Seven brothers and their mother suffered whip and thong, burnings and cuttings, and finally death. Beginning with the eldest, each was made to witness the inhuman sufferings of the others. The mother was the last to die.

While thousands of martyr-saints were proving their belief in the future life of blessedness, others bravely rallied to the cry of the priest Mathathias. "If you wish to keep the Law, come, follow me." It was a challenging cry and many obeyed it. Mathathias, supported by his brave sons and sturdy followers, drove the minor officers from their posts, and a local peace was gained. Success stimulated their courage; but Mathathias, a man well up in years, proposed that his sons, the Machabees, substitute for him and he appointed Judas their leader.

Judas Machabeus, a great leader and a warrior, drew his sword and led the revolt. He and his army feared no one. God was with them and through many battles the Syrian army fled before them. Judas in a final encounter against Nicanor, 160 B.C., put an end to long years of suffering. Pagan altars were demolished, the Temple was purified and worship was once more offered to Yahweh. There was great rejoicing.

While from this period on, religion in Judea flourished, still there was little civic peace. Conquests were resumed almost without interruption, until finally in the latter part of the year 63 B. C., Pompey, a Roman general, took control of Jerusalem and all Palestine in the name of Emperor Augustus.

GOD AND THE OLD TESTAMENT

God created the world and placed man above all creatures. Adam's sin changed God's plan toward man, but not His love. He won many back through love, through infinite love.

Adam brought sin into the world, but repentant, he responded to that love; yet the greater number of the children of Adam did not. Noe became one of God's outstanding leaders. And then Abraham followed. In him God selected and blessed above all others, a single people. In the deliverance of the sons of Jacob from the bondage of the Egyptians, a nation, God's Chosen People, was born. Ever after, through leaders, judges, kings and prophets God directed and guided them. Under Moses He made a Covenant with them and later directed Josue in dividing the Promised Land among them. When they wanted a king as ruler, God gave in to their desire. When they became unfaithful, God scattered and purified them.

But in spite of an Almighty God's unfailing fatherly interest, the great, great majority remained unfaithful. 167

God and the Old Testament

Often they turned completely from God to the worship of idols. Under some circumstances they considered it no great evil to worship God, and at the same time, to please friends and neighbors, to give honor to false gods as well.

All God's work among the Jews, however, was not fruitless and not all the Jews were disloyal to Him. Man's redemption was being accomplished. In comparison to the nation as a whole, those who remained faithful were few. The returned exiles from Babylon were but a remnant of the race but they became the heart or core of approved Jewish belief. During their banishment they had been purified and later faced even greater purification. According to God's plan, these selected few laid the foundation of the Holy Land, the scene of the Redeemer's life on earth. Through these few faithful souls the final prophecies were fulfilled. Through these, the final blessings of the Redemption were realized.

God's coming was drawing near. Jesus Christ Our Lord came, and lived among men. The Old Testament ended and the New began.

Personal Record

name _____

born _____
   in _____

baptism _____
   priest _____
   parish _____
   godfather _____
   godmother _____

first communion _____
   priest _____
   parish _____

confirmation _____
   bishop _____
   parish _____
   sponsor _____
   confirmation name _____

Family Record

father _____
    born _____ in _____

mother _____
    born _____ in _____

brothers and sisters _____

_____

father's family
    grandfather _____
        born _____
    grandmother _____
        born _____

mother's family
    grandfather _____
        born _____
    grandmother _____
        born _____

THE NEW TESTAMENT

This is the New Testament, the Covenant or solemn agreement which Christ offers to each soul who will accept it.

The simple stories on the pages which follow are retold from the Gospels written by the Evangelists, Matthew, Mark, Luke and John. These were men who themselves heard Our Lord preach or who had intimate and spiritual relations with Our Lord's Apostles. The Church acknowledges their writings as inspired by the Holy Spirit.

The stories which these holy men left us are the glad tidings of salvation which were brought to earth by the Son of God. They tell the whole ministry of Our Lord's preaching all through Palestine from Galilee to Jerusalem, together with details of His bitter Passion and Death and the glories of His Resurrection.

It is through the inspiration which we receive when we hear or read this sacred legacy, the New Testament, that we learn the heavenly message that helps us to grow ever more like unto Christ Himself.

The Annunciation

Luke 1:26-36

It may have been early evening in spring when Mary, the Virgin Maid of Nazareth, was kneeling at prayer. Suddenly, in a glow of radiant light, the Angel Gabriel, a messenger sent by God, stood before her. In speechless wonder Mary looked at the angel. Then she heard the angel's greeting, "Hail, full of grace, the Lord is with thee. Blessed art thou among women." Mary was troubled. Fear came upon her at the angel's word. Mary kept pondering in her heart what manner of greeting this might be.

The angel said, "Fear not, Mary, for you have found grace with God. Behold you shall conceive in your womb and shall bring forth a Son and you shall call His name Jesus. He shall be great and shall be called the Son of the Most High. The Lord God shall give to Him the throne of David His Father and He shall reign in the house of Jacob forever. Of His kingdom there shall be no end."

Mary understood the meaning of the angel's message. How could she become the Mother of God? She had promised herself as a virgin to a man whose name was Joseph. Mary said to the angel, "How shall this be done because I know not man?"

The angel told Mary that the Holy Spirit would come upon her and the power of the Most High would overshadow her. The angel told her also that the Holy Child which would be born of her would be the Son of God. And then the angel added, "And behold, your cousin Elizabeth, in her old age, will have a son and this is the sixth month with her. No word is impossible with God."

Then Mary said, "Behold the handmaid of the Lord; be it done to me according to Your word." At the moment that Mary pronounced this simple acceptance of God's will, she became the Mother of God. The Word was made flesh and lived within her.

The angel departed but Mary knelt in long, quiet adoration of God Who had now become Man in order to save mankind.

The Visitation

THE VISITATION

Luke 1:39-56

In the days that followed the angel's visit, Mary rose up and went in all haste to the hill country where Zachary lived.

Entering the house, Mary greeted Elizabeth. No sooner had Elizabeth heard Mary's greeting than she was filled with the Holy Ghost. With a loud, jubilant voice she said, "Blessed are you among women and blessed is the fruit of your womb. How have I deserved to be visited by the Mother of my Lord? Blessed are you because you have believed. The message you have received shall be fulfilled."

And Mary said gloriously but humbly:

"My soul magnifies the Lord,
and my spirit rejoices in God my Savior,

Because He has regarded the lowliness of His handmaid,
for behold, henceforth all generations
shall call me blessed,

Because He Who is mighty has done great things for me,
and holy is His name;

And His mercy is from generation to generation
toward those who fear Him.

He has shown might with His arm;
He has scattered the proud in the conceit of their
heart.

He has put down the mighty from their thrones
and has exalted the lowly.

The hungry He has filled with good things
and the rich He has sent empty away.

He has given help to Israel His servant
mindful of His mercy —

As He promised our fathers —
toward Abraham and his descendants forever."

And Mary stayed with Elizabeth about three months, and then returned to her own home in Nazareth.

177

The Birth of Jesus

Luke 2

Several months after the return of Mary to Nazareth, Joseph brought Mary, his promised wife, to live with him. Joseph knew from the message of an angel that Mary carried within her the Lord of heaven and earth Who in time would be born of her. Mary's heart and all the thoughts of her mind were fixed on God and the great blessings which had come to her. The months passed quietly and serenely in their modest home.

And then one day the peace of the town was disturbed. Cæsar Augustus, the great emperor of Rome, through his governor Cyrinus, announced that a census would be made. For it, each citizen was to go to the town of his birth and register there. It did not matter that traveling was inconvenient to Mary. God's will was expressed through the exact demand of the law. In obedience, then, to the imperial decree, Joseph and Mary gathered together a few necessities for the journey and set out. After weary traveling of four or five days, they reached Bethlehem. Joseph immediately sought for lodging, but there was none to be had. There was no room for them in the inns.

Night had already fallen when Mary and Joseph found shelter in a cave. Here in the midst of the silent night Mary brought forth the Babe Who was Christ the Lord. Mary knelt in deepest adoration before her Son Who was the great God of heaven and earth. Joseph joined Mary in silent prayer. God had come, a tiny Babe, to live among men. The Word, the Promise of God the Father, was made Flesh and dwelt among us.

The Shepherds

Luke 2:8-20

In the fields not far from the cave where Christ was born, shepherds were keeping night watch over their flocks. They were terrified when suddenly the sky was filled with light and an angel said to them, "Do not be afraid, for behold, I bring you good news of great joy which shall be to all people; for today in the town of David, a Savior has been born to you Who is Christ the Lord." That they might recognize Him, the angel gave them a sign: "You will find an Infant wrapped in winding bands and lying in a manger."

Then a host of angels joined the heavenly messenger and the night was made joyous with angelic song: "Glory to God in the highest and peace on earth to men of good will."

After the angels departed and the echo of their song had died away, the shepherds went in haste to search for the Child. They found Mary and Joseph and the Babe lying in the manger.

And when they had seen, they understood what had been told them concerning the Child. With simple faith they believed the message they had heard from the angels.

From the shepherds Mary learned of the appearance of the angels and of their song of glory. But she kept silent about these wonders, thinking over them in her heart. And the shepherds returned to their flocks glorifying and praising God for all the things they had heard and seen.

The Presentation

THE PRESENTATION

Luke 2:22-39

Forty days after our Savior's birth, Mary, carrying Jesus in her arms, accompanied by Joseph, set out for Jerusalem.

The Law required that people of wealth offer a lamb and a turtle dove. But Mary brought two pigeons, the usual offering of the poor. On entering the temple, Mary ascended the staircase of the Women's Court and prostrated herself in humble prayer. Shortly thereafter, a priest came to her and accepted the two pigeons for a sacrifice to the Most High God. This was the ceremony of Purification. Later in the Priests' Court the blood of these pigeons was poured out over the Altar of Burnt-Offerings.

Immediately the ceremony of Presentation followed. Now it must be understood that the first-born son of Jewish parents was considered the Lord's, because at the time when the Jews had left Egypt, God spared the first-born male child of every Jewish family. In keeping with this ceremony, then, Mary presented her first-born Son to the priest, who, according to the Jewish ceremony, took Jesus in his arms and blessed Him. The ransom prescribed for the return of the Child was five shekels. The Holy Family having paid this, the Child was given back.

As the Holy Family was leaving after the ceremony, there came toward them a venerable old man, Simeon, who under the inspiration of the Holy Spirit recognized the Babe in Mary's arms as the Promised Messias. Reverently he took the Child in his arms and exclaimed prophetically:

"Now, Lord, dismiss your servant
in peace, according to your word;
For my eyes have seen Your salvation,
which You have set before all the nations,
As a light of revelation for the Gentiles
and the glory of Your people Israel."

And then Simeon turned to Mary and continued his prophetic words:

"Behold, this Child is destined for the fall and for the rise of many in Israel and for a sign that shall be

183

The Three Wise Men

contradicted. And your own soul a sword shall pierce, that the thoughts of many hearts may be revealed." Simeon's song of joy, followed by his austere prophetic words, revealed to Mary a strong and frightening vision, the conflict that would arise for all time between good and evil because of the teachings of her Son. He was to be the "Man of Sorrows" and she the "Mother of Sorrows." Indeed at that moment Mary's heart was spiritually pierced with a sharp sword of sorrow.

While Simeon was still speaking, Anna, a woman of great age and a prophetess, also joined the crowd which had gathered. Anna spoke of the wonders of God to such as were ready to accept the Redemption of Israel.

THE THREE WISE MEN

Matthew 2:1-12

A large, richly outfitted caravan of camels, directed by three distinguished men called "Magi," and a retinue of servants, moved into Jerusalem. As they made their way into the city, a crowd gathered around them. The question of the Magi, "Where is He that is born King of the Jews?" created surprise and wonder. When Herod heard the question of the Magi, he not only wondered but was much troubled because he feared for his own throne. Immediately he decided that he would make every effort to find this new King and then do away with Him.

Hurriedly, Herod assembled the chief priests and scribes. These men knew the prophecy of Micheas and at once told Herod, "This King is to be born in Bethlehem of Judea."

In a secret interview, Herod told the Magi where to find the newborn King, and then inquired from them when the star first appeared and how long they had been on the way. He wanted to get some idea of the age of this new King. Then in deceitful and sacrilegious words he told the Magi to return after they had found this Infant King for he, too, wished to pay Him homage.

185

The Flight into Egypt

Satisfied and happy that they were at length at the end of their journey and about to see this heavenly Child, the Magi resumed their traveling. Great was their joy for as soon as they left Jerusalem, the star they had seen in the east, directed them once more.

The Holy Family no longer lived in a cave but had moved to a modest little home in Bethlehem over which the star soon rested. The King they sought lived in no palace and looked as any ordinary child might look. Supernaturally guided by God's Spirit and enlightened in heart and mind, these holy men knew that the light that had appeared in the East and had guided them to Bethlehem was no ordinary star, and the Child they saw was no ordinary child. They knew they were in the presence of the Messias Who would enlighten both Jew and Gentile. They knelt and adored the Infant King and offered their gifts of gold, frankincense and myrrh.

During the night, in a dream, the Magi were directed not to return to Herod, but to go back to their own countries by a different route. Herod's plan was defeated.

THE FLIGHT INTO EGYPT

Matthew 2:13-15

Herod waited and waited for the return of the Magi. He finally concluded that they had out-witted him. He was filled with anxiety and rage and his wicked mind worked rapidly. He sent his soldiers into the quiet little town of Bethlehem to kill every male child two years old and under. Possibly forty or more little ones were put to the sword. There was loud weeping and lamentation throughout all Bethlehem.

But the Christ Child was safe. An angel had ap-peared to Joseph during the night, very likely the night of the visit of the Magi, and told him to go to Egypt with the Child and His mother because Herod had in mind to kill the Child. Unnoticed, Joseph and Mary and the Child left Bethlehem under the cover of darkness. The journey took from five to six days.

Jesus Is Found in the Temple

There were many Jewish settlements in Egypt where the Holy Family could have felt secure away from the reach of Judea's wicked tyrant and sheltered from danger. History does not give the exact spot where they stayed.

After the death of Herod, which according to history occurred but a short time later, Joseph was again told by an angel in a dream to return. There is reason to believe that Joseph had intended to settle in Bethlehem, his own birthplace. On reaching the borders of Judea, however, he learned that Herod's wicked son, Archelaus, was ruling over the territory. Jesus would not be safe there. Joseph's fears were eased by another message from an angel. Nazareth, where Mary's people lived, belonged to Antipas who was better liked by the people. So, acting on the word of the angel, the Holy Family went back to Nazareth where Jesus was to live for thirty years.

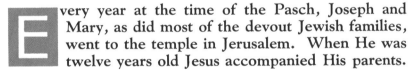

JESUS IS FOUND IN THE TEMPLE

Luke 2:41-52

Every year at the time of the Pasch, Joseph and Mary, as did most of the devout Jewish families, went to the temple in Jerusalem. When He was twelve years old Jesus accompanied His parents.

After the solemn feast was over, Joseph and Mary in company with their relatives and friends, started the return trip to Nazareth, but Jesus, all unknown to them, remained in Jerusalem. The party had come a day's journey before Jesus was missed. Confused and full of grief and anxiety, Mary and Joseph retraced their steps toward Jerusalem.

For two days the sorrowful couple searched with aching hearts throughout the length and breadth of the big, crowded city for their lost Child. Then on the third day they went to the temple. There they saw Him sitting and talking with the Doctors of the Law. Seeing Him they were filled with joy but they could not understand. Mary, following the impulse of her aching heart, ran to Him and embraced Him. "Son," she said touchingly,

Jesus Is Baptized

"why have You done so to us? In great sorrow Your father and I have been looking for You."

Jesus looked at His parents lovingly and then gave them an answer that made them wonder. "How is it that you sought Me?" He replied. "Did you not know that I must be about My Father's business?"

Until this happening Jesus had always acted as any other child might act. But this incident gave His parents a strange feeling that He had grown up. Knowing Him to be God and Savior of the world, they began to realize that He would have to suffer to save it.

But Jesus went down with them to Nazareth and was obedient to them. And then for eighteen years He led a hidden life. But often during these years Mary thought over the words that Jesus had said, for she kept them always in her heart.

The Gospel sums up these years of Our Lord by saying, "He grew in wisdom and age and grace before God and men."

JESUS IS BAPTIZED
Luke 3:1-21

The Gospel tells us that "The Word of the Lord," that is, the inspiration to teach God's message, "came to John, son of Zachary, in the desert. He came unto the Jordan, preaching the baptism of penance for the remission of sin."

John's preaching aroused a spirit of expectation among his hearers so that they wondered if he perhaps were not the Christ, that is, the Messias for Whom they were waiting. John told them he was not but said to them, "There is One to come Who is greater than I am, the strap of Whose shoe I am not worthy to loose."

The fame of John's preaching spread throughout Judea so that one day it even reached the little village of Nazareth. When Jesus learned of it, He knew that this was the moment set by His heavenly Father to begin His public life. He parted from His dear Mother and set out toward the Jordan with a small group on a pilgrimage of penance.

When they reached the Jordan, Christ and His companions waited in line to be baptized. Now John knew that the Messias would one day come to the Jordan, and when in turn Jesus stood in the water before him, by an inspiration from on high he recognized Christ. John said, "It is I who ought to be baptized by You, and do You come to me?"

Humbly, quietly, Christ answered, Let it be so now, for so it is fitting for us to fulfill all justice."

Immediately coming up from the water Christ saw the heavens open and the Holy Ghost in the form of a dove descended upon Him and a voice from heaven was heard saying, "This is My beloved Son in Whom I am well pleased."

The great moment of John's work was the baptism of Christ. In this baptism John completed his own public ministry. By the same act, the baptism of Christ, God the Father solemnly approved the ministry of His beloved Son as the Messias, and the New Testament replaced the Old. After this solemn ceremony of Christ many of John's disciples associated themselves with Christ.

THE DEVIL TEMPTS JESUS

Luke 4:1-13

After the baptism in the Jordan, the Spirit led Jesus into the desert for the space of forty days. In this lonely, parched and mountainous wasteland, by prayer and fasting, Our Lord prepared Himself to preach and also to meet the assaults of Satan.

When the days of fasting were at an end and Christ was physically weak, He was approached in the wilderness by Satan in the guise of a young man who said, "If You are the Son of God, command that these stones become loaves of bread."

Christ looked at the stones at His feet and then raising His eyes, looked at Satan and without revealing His divinity said, "Not in bread alone does man live, but in every word that proceeds from the mouth of God."

The answer, though disappointing, did not discourage Satan. Continuing his quest, he took Jesus to the pinnacle of the temple and said, "If You are the Son of God, cast Yourself down, for it is written: 'He has given His angels charge over You, and in their hands they will bear You up so that You will not dash Your foot against a stone.'"

Jesus answered, "It is written: 'Tempt not the Lord your God.'" Thus again, Christ overcame the temptation as any mere man might have done. Satan was still uncertain.

Vexed, he made a third attempt. In a moment of time, he took Christ up to a high mountain and showed Him all the kingdoms of the world and promised to give Him the power and the glory of them all, if He would adore him. Jesus answered that God alone was worthy of adoration. Satan was still confused but made no more attacks on this God-fearing Man until the final battle of the Passion.

Consolingly for us who are also tempted, the Gospel ends this story: "And behold, angels came and ministered unto Him."

John 1:35-51

Now John the Baptist knew that Jesus was about to begin His public life and was expecting that soon He would make a public appearance. And then, it happened one day that Jesus passed by while John was speaking with Andrew and another disciple, very likely John who later would be known as the Evangelist. The Baptist suggested that they follow Jesus. The two disciples walked after Jesus for some distance when He turned and said, "What do you want of Me?"

In response they questioned, "Master, where do you live?"

"Come and see," was the reply. And they stayed with Jesus that day.

Later Andrew met his brother Simon and with great enthusiasm said, "Simon, we have found the Messias." When Andrew brought Simon to Jesus, Jesus looked searchingly at him and without an introduction said, "You are Simon, son of John. You shall be called Peter." The word "Peter" means "a rock."

Philip of Galilee who was also to be one of the twelve was drawn into the ranks by the simple invitation of Jesus, "Follow Me."

Now Nathanael, a good man and a friend of Philip, when he heard about Jesus and his followers, would not be moved. He said, "Can anything good come from Nazareth?" But, in spite of his objection, Nathanael did go with Philip to meet Jesus. On seeing him, Jesus praised him for his straightforwardness and told him that He had seen him under the fig tree before Philip spoke with him. Astounded and completely convinced, Nathanael exclaimed, "You are the Son of God, the King of Israel."

The Wedding Feast at Cana

John 2:1-11

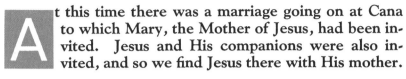t this time there was a marriage going on at Cana to which Mary, the Mother of Jesus, had been invited. Jesus and His companions were also invited, and so we find Jesus there with His mother.

While the feast was in progress, Mary noticed that there was a shortage of wine. Knowing her Son's great power and wishing to save the young couple embarrassment, she said to Jesus, "Son, they have no wine."

Jesus answered, "Woman, what is that to Me and to you? My hour has not yet come."

Though His hour had not yet come, His mother knew that Jesus would grant her request. She said to the waiters, "Do whatever He tells you."

Nearby there were six waterpots. Jesus said to the servants, "Fill these with water."

When the pots were filled, Jesus said to them, "Draw out now, and take to the chief steward." And they took it to him. Now when the chief steward had tasted the water after it had become wine, not knowing whence it was (though the attendants who had drawn the water knew), the chief steward called the bridegroom and said to him, "Everyman at first sets forth good wine, and when they have drunk freely, then that which is poorer, but you have kept the good wine until now."

This first of His signs Jesus worked at Cana of Galilee; and He manifested His glory and the disciples believed in Him. After this He went down to Capharnaum, He and His mother, and His brethren, and His disciples. And they stayed there a few days.

The Sellers in the Temple

THE SELLERS IN THE TEMPLE

Matthew 21:12-13

Saint Matthew tells us that Capharnaum was Christ's own town. In Our Lord's day it was well populated and easily reached by roads which led both east and west. It was picturesque, built against wooded hills, on the edge of the blue water of Lake Genesareth. Seemingly the beauty of this lake had strong attractions for Christ. Many times He taught the multitudes on its shores and often, both by day and by night, He with His disciples, sailed its cool waters. In the Gospel stories, the lake is also referred to as the Sea of Tiberius or the Sea of Galilee. If Christ loved the natural beauty of this spot, He loved its people more, for they above all others heard more of His sacred teaching.

After the wedding at Cana, Christ and His disciples and His mother and her relatives went down to Capharnaum and remained there a few days. Here they prepared to leave on a pilgrimage to Jerusalem to celebrate the Pasch. For this feast all roads to Jerusalem were thronged with faithful Jews, full of joy that once again they might enter the Holy City and offer sacrifice in their magnificent temple.

When Christ entered Solomon's porch He saw a bewildering sight. Buyers, sellers and money-changers were loud and intent upon their bargainings. There was confusion and uproar. Indignation and holy anger filled the heart of Christ. He made a whip of cords and with it drove these desecrators from His Father's house. Stunned, they made no resistance. Sellers and their animals with them ran in panic before Christ's flashing eyes and upraised arm. He released the doves and overturned the tables of the money-changers. His voice was heard above the din, "Get these things out. Do not make the house of My Father a den of thieves."

The guilty priests were indignant at the authority Christ took upon Himself. And even though in their hearts they knew His action was right, they asked Him angrily, "By what authority have You done this?"

Christ looked at them calmly and gave them a reply which was above their understanding but one which they

Jesus at Jacob's Well

held against Him even to Calvary: "Destroy this temple and in three days I will raise it up."

By "this temple" Christ was referring to His own Body which He would raise up on the third day after the Jews had put Him to death.

They did not dare say more to Him that day. When evening came, Christ left the city.

JESUS AT JACOB'S WELL
John 4:1-42

The hostility of the priests in the temple forced Jesus to leave Judea. He and His apostles set out for Galilee taking the road through Samaria. At noon, after walking up the mountain roads, they reached Jacob's well. Jesus rested there while the apostles went into the city to buy food.

A woman came to the well to draw water. Jesus said to her, "Give Me to drink." Now according to custom, a Jew never addressed a Samaritan, because the two groups, though distinctly related, had become bitter enemies.

Surprised, the woman said, "How is it that You being a Jew, ask water from a Samaritan?"

Looking at her, Jesus said, "If you knew the gift of God and Who It is Who is asking you for water, you would perhaps ask for living water."

"Sir," she replied, "how can You give me water? You have nothing wherewith to draw water."

Then Jesus said, "Whoever drinks this water will thirst again, but he who drinks the water I shall give him will not thirst forever."

The woman's quick reply was, "Give me this living water so that I shall never need to come here to draw water."

Jesus challenged her. "Go," He said, "call your husband and come here."

Thunderstruck, at first the woman said she had no husband, but when she learned that Jesus knew that she had five husbands, she admitted that He was a prophet

201

The Miraculous Draught of Fishes

and then cunningly changed the subject. "Where are we to worship," she asked, "here in Samaria or in Jerusalem?"

The answer came with gentleness and love, "Woman, believe Me, the hour is coming when neither here nor in Jerusalem will you worship the Father. Salvation is from the Jews, but the time is already come when true worshipers will worship the Father in Spirit and in Truth."

This reply reminded the woman of the expected Messias. She said, "I know the Messias is coming and when He comes He will tell us all things."

Jesus then revealed Himself to her, "I Who speak with you am He."

She believed; her conversion was complete. Putting her pitcher down, she ran into the city to invite her townsfolk to come and see Jesus.

In the meantime the apostles returned, but Jesus was no longer interested in material food. Instead He spoke to the apostles of the food for which souls were hungering. For two days He dispensed this heavenly food to the simple folk of Samaria who welcomed Him to their city.

THE MIRACULOUS DRAUGHT OF FISHES
Luke 5:1-11

One morning late in May, while Jesus was near Capharnaum, walking along the shore of Lake Genesareth, a crowd, anxious to hear His word, pressed around Him. Nearby were two fishing boats. He went into the one that was Peter's and asked him to move the ship from the shore. Jesus, sitting in the boat, addressed the people.

When He had finished speaking, He said to Peter, "Put out into the deep and lower the nets for a draught."

Peter was reluctant to do it. He replied that he and his partners had been out all night and had caught nothing and then added, "But at Your word, I will lower the nets."

In moments the nets were filled with fish. The catch was so great that the nets were near to breaking. Peter

The Sermon on the Mount

signaled his partners to bring the other boat. The catch filled both boats almost to a point of sinking.

Seeing what had happened, fear came upon the fishermen, and Peter falling to his knees cried out, "Depart from me for I am a sinful man, O Lord."

Then Jesus, easing the fear that came upon Peter and his companions, gave Peter a very meaningful reply. He said, "Fear not. Come after Me and from now on you will catch men."

When they came to shore, the fishermen were men changed in heart and mind. They all understood the invitation which their leader, Peter, received. They, too, would become fishers of men. Encouraged in their desire by Jesus, Andrew, brother of Peter, and James and John his partners, left all things—their homes, their boats and nets—and followed Jesus.

THE SERMON ON THE MOUNT
Matthew 5

The Christian way of living comes because of two sets of laws; the first came from Moses given to him directly by God on Mount Sinai; the second, the completion and perfection of these laws, was given us by Christ from the Mount of the Beatitudes.

The supreme authority to direct man toward his eternal goal which is heaven, lies in the hands of the Maker of mankind, God. So, when God began to form the Jewish nation, the first nation He formed on earth, He did not neglect them.

One day God had called Moses, their leader, to the top of Mount Sinai and the people had been told to gather about the foot of the mountain. There, surrounded by the clouds of heaven, amid thunder and lightning, Moses and the people, too, had heard the voice of God giving commands that were meant for them and for all people of all times.

"I am the Lord Thy God; thou shalt not have strange gods before Me.

205

"Thou shalt not take the Name of the Lord Thy God in vain.

"Remember thou keep holy the Sabbath day.

"Honor thy father and thy mother.

"Thou shalt not kill.

"Thou shalt not commit adultery.

"Thou shalt not steal.

"Thou shalt not bear false witness against thy neighbor.

"Thou shalt not covet thy neighbor's wife.

"Thou shalt not covet thy neighbor's goods."

God was so careful that each human being should know these commands that He not only gave them to us, but also He planted them in our very heart, so that when we disobey them, a voice in our heart tells us we have done wrong. The better our lives, the stronger that voice becomes. If we sin against it and do not listen to it, the voice in us weakens and eventually remains silent.

After Moses died and hundreds and hundreds of years passed on, the teachers and Doctors of the Law in explaining the Commandments and the Laws of Moses, forgot that the Laws were made to keep people close to God. Instead, these teachers made obeying the Laws so difficult that many of the Jews were inclined to murmur against God.

Jesus in this Sermon on the Mount wanted to change this effect of wrong teaching. His wonderful words of mercy tell us how to live God's way of love. The Beatitudes do not do away with the Commandments. They simply teach us how to live them more perfectly. Jesus, then, having His apostles and a great multitude about Him, spoke to them as well as to all who would afterwards call themselves His followers. He said:

"Blessed are the poor in spirit, for theirs is the kingdom of heaven.

"Blessed are the meek, for they shall possess the land.

"Blessed are they who mourn, for they shall be comforted.

"Blessed are they who hunger and thirst for justice, for they shall be satisfied.

"Blessed are the merciful, for they shall obtain mercy.

"Blessed are the clean of heart, for they shall see God.

"Blessed are the peacemakers, for they shall be called the children of God.

"Blessed are they who suffer persecution for justice' sake, for theirs is the kingdom of heaven.

"Blessed are you when men reproach you, and persecute you, and speak falsely, and say all manner of evil against you for My sake. Rejoice and be glad because your reward is great in heaven, for so did they persecute the prophets who were before you."

Jesus spoke of many more things to His listeners, but this, the great precept of love, was not like anything they had been told before. "You have heard it said, 'Thou shalt love thy neighbor and shalt hate thy enemy.' But I say to you, love your enemies, do good to those who hate you, and pray for those who persecute and calumniate you."

On another occasion Our Lord gave just Two Commandments that contain the whole Law of God. These are:

"First, Thou shalt love the Lord thy God with thy whole heart, with thy whole soul, and with thy whole mind, and with thy whole strength.

"Second, Thou shalt love thy neighbor as thyself."

When Jesus had completely finished His sermon, the people moved away slowly and quietly. His sermon made a deep impression on them. They were astonished and wondered at the things He said. Never had they heard anyone speak as He had spoken.

The Son of the Widow of Naim

Luke 7:11-17

Our Lord with His disciples was starting out on a missionary tour. A large crowd, mostly poor people, followed Him, and no wonder. After the words of His sermon on the Mount spread about, the poor and the suffering knew that He was their friend. Never had they heard such words of sympathy and understanding.

And now as Our Lord moved toward the village of Naim, there came from its gates a mournful sight, a funeral procession. The dead man who was being carried to his grave was the only son of his mother and she was a widow. When Our Lord saw the mother, He was moved to pity and said to her, "Do not weep." Approaching the stretcher, He put His hand on it, and the men carrying it stood still. Then He said, "Young man, I say to you, arise." Immediately the dead man came to life, sat up, and began to speak, and Our Lord, taking him by the hand, gave him to his mother.

The onlookers were overcome with awe and they all began to glorify God saying, "A great prophet is risen up among us: God has visited His people."

This story of Him was told throughout all Judea and all the country around.

The Sinful Woman at Simon's House

Luke 7:36-50

The Pharisees began to wonder among themselves about Jesus and His teachings. They heard of His mercy, His kindness, His love for the poor. They knew, too, that he was not in sympathy with the Scribes and the Pharisees. So, one of their number, Simon by name, invited others of the Pharisees and Jesus to eat at his house. Jesus accepted the invitation.

There was in the city at that time a sinful woman, who, when she had heard that Jesus had gone into Simon's house, pushed her way in and humbly knelt at the feet of Jesus. With her tears she washed His feet and wiped them with her hair. She kissed them and anointed them with costly perfume.

Simon and his guests were disturbed. Simon said within himself: "This Man, were He a prophet, would know who and what sort of woman this is who is touching Him, for she is a sinner."

Jesus turned to Simon and in a kindly manner said, "Simon, I have something to say to you."

Simon answered, "Master, speak."

And Jesus said, "A certain money-lender had two debtors. The one owed him five hundred pieces of silver, the other, fifty. As they had no means of paying, he forgave them both. Which of them will love him more?"

"I suppose," answered Simon, "he to whom he forgave more."

Jesus said, "You have answered rightly." Then he turned to the woman and said to Simon, "Do you see this woman? I came into your house and you gave Me no water for My feet; she has washed My feet with her tears and wiped them with her hair. You gave Me no kiss, but she, from the moment she entered has not ceased to kiss My feet. You did not pour oil on My head; she has anointed My feet. And so I say to you, her sins, many as they are, shall be forgiven her because she has loved much. He loves little who has little forgiven him."

Then speaking to the woman, He said, "Your sins are forgiven. Your faith has saved you. Go in peace."

211

Calming the Tempest

The Pharisees were still far from understanding their Guest. They thought within themselves, "Who is this that forgives sins?"

CALMING THE TEMPEST
Matthew 14:22-33

Jesus had been teaching His hearers through most of the day. When the sun was setting and night falling, He dismissed the crowd and remained in the boat from which He had been speaking. He asked the apostles to raise the sails and make for the eastern shore of the lake.

The lake was calm and the boat moved smoothly over the waters. Jesus being tired lay in the back of the boat, His head resting on a pillow. Soon He was fast asleep.

The apostles were enjoying the sail when in a few brief moments the sky changed. Being well acquainted with the rise of sudden storms on the lake, they became anxious, for by now they had reached the middle of the lake. The heavy winds lashed the waves to terrible heights and their little boat ran the risk of being swallowed up. They had already done all that was possible to save their craft; their courage failed.

During all the roar of wind and wave, Jesus slept serenely. He was now their only hope. Shouting, their cries of fear rose above the din of the storm, "Lord, Jesus, save us. We perish."

Jesus, being thus awakened so suddenly, said reproachfully, "Why are you fearful, O you of little faith?"

Then commanding the wind and the sea, He said, "Peace, be still." At once the wind ceased and there was a great calm so that all in the boat marveled. The amazed apostles said one to the other, "Who is this, for the wind and the sea obey Him?"

213

The Daughter of Jairus

Matthew 9:18-26

In the morning Jesus returned over the lake to the shores of Capharnaum. People had recognized the boat, and a crowd gathered to greet Him.

But suddenly there was a break in the crowd and a distressed man fell on his knees before Jesus. He was Jairus, one of the leaders in the synagogue. "My daughter," he explained, "is at the point of death." And pleading, he went on, "Come, lay Your hand upon her that she may be saved and live."

Jesus was moved by the anguish of the father and started to return with him to his house. The crowd followed them. While on their way, Jesus suddenly asked, "Who touched Me?"

The question surprised everyone but only Peter took courage to remark that in the midst of so great a crowd, many might have touched Him. But Jesus insisted on knowing. He repeated, "Someone has touched Me because power has gone out from Me."

Jesus and those about Him stood still and for a moment nothing happened. Then, timidly, a woman came toward Jesus and knelt at His feet to say that she had touched Him because she felt that if she touched but the hem of His garment she would be cured. She explained that she had been suffering for twelve years from a flow of blood and physicians had not helped her. Jesus looked at her tenderly and said, "Daughter, your faith has saved you. Go in peace."

Jesus had scarcely finished speaking when one of Jairus' servants ran up to his master and said, "Your daughter is dead. Do not trouble the Master."

Turning to the sorrowing father, Jesus said, "Do not be afraid, only have faith and she shall live."

As they drew near the house they heard the confused noise of the mourners. Jesus said, "Why do you make this noise and weep? The girl is asleep, not dead." But they laughed at Him scornfully. When He went into the house all made a move to enter, but He allowed only Peter, James and John and the girl's parents to enter.

Miracle of the Loaves and the Fishes

Taking the dead child's hand, Jesus said, "Child, arise." She arose immediately. All were astounded at Christ's power and love. He commanded all present not to speak of what had taken place.

THE MIRACLE OF THE LOAVES AND THE FISHES

Mark 6:30-44

At Capharnaum Jesus awaited the return of the apostles who had been on their first missionary journey, preaching in neighboring towns and villages. After they had returned and related all things that they had done and taught, Jesus said, "Come apart to a desert place and rest awhile." Jesus had planned to take them across the lake to a desert land near Bethsaida.

The people about Capharnaum seeing whither the boat was heading, kept it in sight as they walked around the shore of the lake. The crowd grew larger and larger. When the boat stopped near Bethsaida, the crowd looked to Jesus for attention. He did not disappoint them; they looked like sheep without a shepherd. The apostles' well-deserved rest was forgotten; the day turned out to be a busy one.

Jesus spoke at great length to the multitude who were most attentive to His every word. The time for noon refreshments had long since passed and the apostles became uneasy. Finally they approached Jesus asking Him to send the crowd into the village to buy food. Jesus answered, "Give you them to eat."

The command astonished them. How could they? They knew that the money they had could not buy enough even to give each person a little. But Jesus knew what He would do and asked, "How many loaves have you?"

Andrew said there was a boy in the crowd that had five barley loaves and two fishes and added, "But what are these among so many?"

Jesus said, "Bring them to Me and make the people sit down."

217

Jesus Walks on the Water

It was in the spring of the year and there was much grass in the place. The people sat down in groups of fifty or a hundred. When the crowd was settled, Jesus took the five loaves and the two fishes into His sacred hands, raised His eyes to heaven, blessed and broke the food and gave it to His apostles to distribute. After all had eaten as much as they wanted, the apostles collected twelve baskets that remained. The crowd numbered five thousand men, not counting women and children.

The people were overcome at so great a miracle. At first they were speechless and then suddenly an acclaim was voiced through all the crowd: "This is indeed the Prophet Who is to come into the world." They would make Him king. In the excitement that was stirred up, Jesus quickly got His apostles into the boat and He Himself went away from the crowd and retired alone into the mountains to pray.

JESUS WALKS ON THE WATER

Mark 6:45-52

The apostles were not pleased about leaving Bethsaida without Jesus but soon a more urgent problem made them forget their disappointment. A strong wind drove them off their course and, experienced fishermen though they were, they made little headway. When early morning broke, they were lost and discouraged.

There was just one path that led from Jesus in Bethsaida to His disheartened apostles and that was over the waters, and He took it. Through the mist of early dawn these struggling fishermen saw a figure moving over the water toward them. They all saw it. As it moved nearer they were terror stricken. They cried, "It is a ghost." Above the noise of the wind and wave there came a familiar and most welcome voice, "Take courage; It is I; do not be afraid."

Their fear was at an end. With Jesus there, they knew all their troubles were over. Peter, impulsive and always wanting to be near the Master he loved, called out, "If it be You, Lord, bid me come to You upon the water."

219

Jesus said, "Come." Immediately Peter stepped down upon the water and walked toward the approaching figure. But suddenly he became conscious of what he was doing and his courage failed and he cried out, "Lord, save me!" Jesus extended His hand to Peter and said, "Oh, you of little faith. Why did you doubt?"

They both entered the ship; the wind stopped and in moments the boat reached shore.

JESUS TESTS THE FAITH OF HIS FOLLOWERS

Mark 8:11-21

The morning after the multiplication of the loaves, some of the crowd which had remained in Bethsaida, were seeking Jesus. They were still bent on making Him king. Not finding Him there, they decided to take a chance at finding Him in Capharnaum and boarded the fishing boats that were lying idle, and had the fishermen sail them across the lake.

They were right. They soon met Jesus and inquired of Him how He had returned to Capharnaum. Our Lord knew their hearts. He did not answer their question but told them that they were seeking Him not because of the miracles they had seen Him work, but because they had been fed with the loaves and were filled. He tried to raise their thoughts and desires to higher things. He said, "Do not work for the food that perishes but for that which will last forever, which the Son of Man will give you. For upon Him the Father, God Himself, has set His seal."

His audience knew that He was speaking about something which had higher value than ordinary food of the body and that there was a way for them to get this better Food. They desired to have it, for they asked, "What work must we do to obtain this Food?"

The answer was clear, "This is the work of God, that you believe in Him Whom He has sent." They knew He was referring to Himself as the One sent from the Father, but they were not ready with the act of faith which He required. They wanted further proof. They asked, "What sign can You give us that we may see and believe?"

220

They had just been witnesses to the great miracle of the multiplication of the loaves. This to them was not enough. Had not Moses done as much and more? "Our fathers," they said, "ate the manna in the desert, even as it is written, 'He gave them bread from heaven to eat.'"

Our Lord then distinguished between two breads, the bread that supports the natural life and another bread far superior, a spiritual food which only His Father can give. Then in great earnestness He said, "Believe Me when I tell you this: the bread that comes from heaven is not what Moses gave you. The real bread from heaven is given only by My Father. God's gift of bread comes down from heaven and gives life to the world."

It is very likely that His hearers did not fully understand the greatness of this true bread. But they did understand that It was different from ordinary bread and was to be very much desired and they asked for It, "Give us always this bread."

And now the moment came for Jesus to test the faith and confidence of the multitudes that followed Him. He had given proof upon proof that He was the Son of Man, sent by His Father in heaven. It was for them to decide now whether they believed in Him or not. He would have only believers. This was His Father's will. Jesus said clearly and positively, "I am the bread of life. He who comes to Me shall not hunger, and he who believes in Me shall never thirst... for I am come down from heaven... this is the will of My Father Who sent Me, that whoever beholds the Son, and believes in Him, shall have everlasting life, and I will raise him up on the last day."

These words left no room for doubt but scandalized most of His hearers. The Scribes and the Pharisees were loud in their mutterings: "Is not this Jesus, Son of Joseph, Whose father and mother we know? How then does He say, 'I have come down from heaven?'"

The dissension deeply hurt the Heart of Jesus and He knew that most of them would come to Him no more, but He did not change the meaning of His words to them. He said, "Do not murmur among yourselves." Then with an oath He added, "Amen, Amen, I say to you, he who believes in Me has life everlasting."

The Promise of the Blessed Sacrament

John 6:25-70

And now Jesus came to something very strange and very wonderful. "I am the bread of life... I am the living bread that has come down from heaven," He said. "If anyone eat this bread he shall live forever; and the bread that I will give is My flesh for the life of the world."

The insistence of Christ provoked a heated discussion among the unbelievers, the Scribes, Pharisees and Jews who had come from Jerusalem. They asked each other in their complete disbelief, "How can this Man give us His flesh to eat?"

Jesus did not change anything that He had said. Again He spoke most emphatically, "Amen, Amen, I say to you, unless you eat the flesh of the Son of Man and drink His blood, you shall not have life in you. He who eats My flesh and drinks My blood has Life everlasting, and I will raise him up on the last day. For My flesh is food indeed and My blood is drink indeed."

The multitude who disbelieved asked, "How can this *Man* give us His flesh to eat?" They took Jesus for a mere man. No man could do what He had promised. But Jesus was not mere man. In His statement He called Himself the *Son of Man*, which meant God, Son of the Father and sent by Him. His hearers had this knowledge, but they would not admit the truth. They would not believe that Jesus was God.

And Jesus would not change what He had promised. It was always His way when people misunderstood, to explain further, but when He was understood and not believed, He merely repeated what He had said. And so He did here. He repeated the same truth over and over but He would not change it. He was going to give them His flesh as true food for their souls.

Jesus was here introducing the doctrine of the Holy Eucharist and the teaching of it caused Jesus much pain because many of His disciples left Him and His enemies became more bitter.

Later, when He was alone with His apostles, He said to them sorrowfully, "Do you also wish to go away?"

Jesus and the Pharisees

Peter answered His question with earnestness and faith, "Lord, to whom shall we go? You have the words of eternal life." Thus Peter declared what Catholics have always declared, "We do not understand how You are going to do it, but we do understand that You have said that You are going to give us Your flesh to eat. Your word is enough for us. God cannot tell a lie, and You are God."

JESUS AND THE PHARISEES
Matthew 12:38-45

A change came. Capharnaum seemed to be the city of Our Lord's choice. Of all the good tidings He had to teach, that pertaining to the gift of His own body and blood to the world, was dearest to His Heart. As He had done, His plan was to give the first news of it to His many disciples and followers at Capharnaum. But for them it proved a hard saying and they did not accept it. It created a break in their friendship. The Heart of Jesus was sorely hurt at the rejection of His gift. He with His apostles left Capharnaum for Tyre and Sidon. Here for a few months they brought joy and consolation to the Gentiles.

On His return to Capharnaum Christ found that the Scribes, Pharisees and Sadducees there, had taken advantage of the attitude of the people against His doctrine. Now whenever the few who still remained faithful came to Jesus, a group of hecklers always appeared to sow discord. They raised questions about ceremonial washings, the observance of the Sabbath and such topics. Each time Our Lord not only overcame their objections, but took the occasion to emphasize a point of His new teaching. Once He said, "But the things that proceed out of the mouth come from the heart, and it is these that defile a man. For out of the heart come evil thoughts, murders, adulteries, immorality, theft, false witnesses, blasphemies. These are the things that defile a man; but to eat with unwashed hands does not defile a man."

In spite of the defeat to all their arguments, these men of the Law were determined to conquer their foe.

225

Peter is Made Head of the Church

They said, "Give us, if you can, a positive proof of what you claim." Jesus could see their hearts which were full of malice toward Him; they were wilfully blind. Had they been of good will they would have read the signs of Christ's divinity in the supernatural works He had already done among the people. Patiently the Lord gave them a reply, "You read the message of the skies. You know by it when to expect rain and when the weather will be fair. Can you not read the signs of the times?" Jesus sighed deeply in the spirit and then finished: "Why does this generation ask a sign? It is a wicked and unfaithful generation and a sign shall not be given it."

PETER IS MADE HEAD OF THE CHURCH
Matthew 16:13-20

After Our Lord had been teaching for awhile, He had picked out twelve from among His followers to share more intimately with Him His plan for spreading the Kingdom of God on earth. These He called "Apostles" which means sent out on a mission. Once He sent them out two by two to preach to the people. He even gave them the power to work miracles.

They had just now traveled with Him over the lake from Capharnaum to Bethsaida along the Jordan River toward Mount Hermon. Here at the foot of the mountain, at Cæsarea Philippi, Jesus and His apostles spent a few days in prayer and solitude.

One day as Jesus walked along the road with them, He suddenly broke off the conversation to ask, "Who do men say the Son of Man is?"

The question was so abrupt that it rather startled the apostles. From the various answers He received, Jesus learned that some people believed Him to be John the Baptist returned to life; others thought He might be Elias and others Jeremias or one of the prophets. Not anyone of the apostles mentioned that He was thought to be the Messias. To the ordinary Jew, the Messias would be an outstanding world leader and their Jerusalem would be his capital. And yet, this Man of excep-

The Transfiguration

tional spiritual and God-like powers, holy and simple, seemed not to want civil authority. They were perplexed. They had no idea of a spiritual kingdom over the hearts of men.

Jesus now would test the apostles themselves. What was their thought of Him? He asked, "But Who do you say I am?"

Peter's answer was prompt and awe-inspiring: "Thou art the Christ, the Son of the living God." It was a magnificent act of the deepest faith.

Our Lord's appreciative response was one of kingly trust, "Blessed are you, Simon-Bar-Jona, for flesh and blood has not revealed this to you, but My Father in heaven." And then followed the great promise of the founding of the Church: "And I say to you, you are Peter, and upon this rock I will build My Church, and the gates of hell shall not prevail against it. And I will give you the keys of the kingdom of Heaven; and whatever you shall bind on earth shall be bound in heaven, and whatever you shall loose on earth shall be loosed in heaven."

In three word-pictures, Jesus had shown that this man, a rock-like foundation, the keeper of the keys, and the ruler, was to be the head of His Church.

THE TRANSFIGURATION
Matthew 17:1-8

Satisfied that the apostles believed Him to be the Son of the living God and knowing that this faith would be put to the test, Jesus prepared them for it. He told them, "I must go to Jerusalem and suffer many things from the ancients and the Scribes and the chief priests, and be put to death and on the third day rise again." They were horrified. Being Jews and especially Jews of their day who looked for a Messias of great military power, they could not grasp what Jesus was trying to make them understand. He was their leader; He must lead them to victory. But their way to victory was not Christ's.

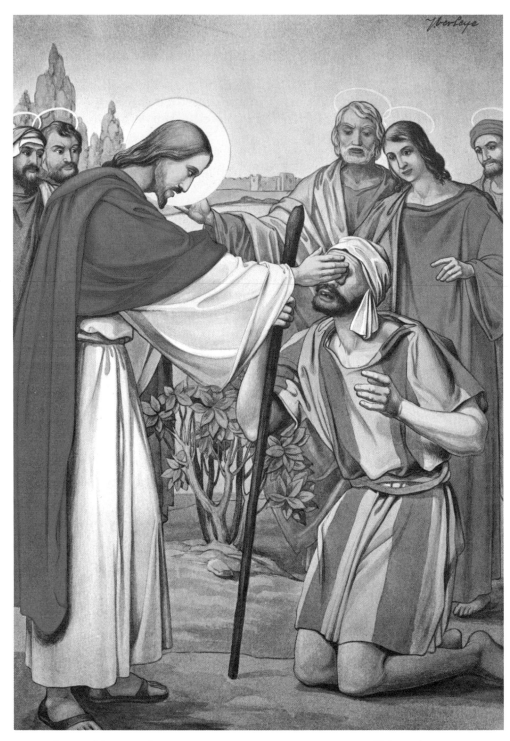

The Cure of the Man Born Blind

Jesus continued to impress this difficult lesson with great sympathy but with persistence. They would have to learn what Jesus already knew so well: the way of the cross is the way to glory. Sorrow now; joy later.

Six days later, Jesus ascended Mount Thabor with His three favorite apostles, Peter, James and John. When they reached the rounded summit Jesus became transfigured before His astonished apostles. As He prayed, the appearance of His face changed. His garments became radiantly white. None of the Evangelists speak of an external light. There was an inner brilliance which radiated from His divine nature and shone out through His Body. Two men, Moses and Elias, appeared in glory and spoke with Jesus about His Passion.

The three apostles were filled with awe, and Peter cried out, "Lord, it is good for us to be here. If You will, let us set up three tents here, one for You, one for Moses and one for Elias."

As Peter was still speaking, a bright cloud overshadowed them and a voice from the cloud said, "This is My beloved Son in Whom I am well pleased; hear Him."

Fearful, the apostles, hearing the voice, fell to the ground. The vision was over swiftly. Jesus touched them and said, "Arise, do not be afraid."

Lifting up their eyes they saw no one but Jesus only.

On the way down from the mountain, Jesus told them to tell the vision to no one until the Son of Man should be risen from the dead. They had seen His glory as God!

THE CURE OF THE MAN BORN BLIND

John 9

After the Transfiguration, Jesus returned from Mount Thabor to Capharnaum accompanied by His apostles. During the weeks that followed, Our Lord gave most of His time to instructing His apostles. The twelve asked questions of Jesus, and after His death the Evangelists in their writings recorded many of these instructions for us in parables. Especially during this time Jesus showed them the need of humility and told them how to practice it.

In late summer Jesus planned that His apostles would go up to Jerusalem for the Feast of the Tabernacles. First Our Lord said He would not go, but later, when the Feast was already half over, He appeared in the temple to teach. At no time during His talks did the Scribes and the Pharisees allow Him any peace. They constantly murmured and argued against His teaching.

One day Jesus with His apostles was passing along the south side of the temple when they noticed a blind man begging. "Rabbi," the apostles asked, "has this man or his parents sinned that he should be born blind?"

Jesus answered, "Neither has this man sinned nor his parents but that the works of God may be made known." Then, spitting on the ground, He made clay of the spittle and spread the clay over the eyes of the young beggar and said, "Go, wash in the pool of Siloe."

The beggar obeyed promptly. He went, washed and returned, seeing.

His neighbors and those who were accustomed to see him begging were confused when they met him cured. Some said, "Is not this the blind man who sat begging?" Others said, "No, it is not he, but he is like him." But the man's positive and joyous answer, "I am he," removed all doubt. They were curious then to know how this came about. He told them in few words just what had happened: "This man called Jesus," he said, "made clay and anointed my eyes and said to me, 'Go to the pool of Siloe and wash;' and I went; I washed; I see."

These neighbors and friends thought that this most unusual happening should be brought to the attention of the Doctors of the Law. They, therefore, brought the cured man to the Pharisees, who asked him how his eyes had been opened. Again he gave his very simple explanation: "Jesus put clay on my eyes, and I washed and I see."

Now it was the Sabbath day on which this had been done. The Pharisees completely disregarded the miracle and said, "This Man is not of God, for He does not keep the Sabbath." But there were others among them, not so prejudiced, that raised the question, "How can a man who is a sinner work such wonders?" And they began to argue among themselves. The angered Pharisees turned to the man who had been cured and questioned, "What do you say of Him who opened your eyes?"

Without hesitation he replied, "He is a prophet."

The Pharisees were determined to deny the truth of this miracle. They sent for the parents of the man who had been cured, to find out if he really had been blind at all. They said to them, "Is this your son, of whom you say he was born blind? How then does he see now?"

The parents answered cautiously, "We know that this is our son and that he was born blind. But how he now sees, we do not know, nor do we know who has opened his eyes. Ask him. He is of age. He can speak for himself." The parents answered so because they were afraid of the priests for they had already agreed that if any man should declare that Jesus was the promised Messias, he would be put out of the synagogue.

Once more these officers of the Law called the man who had been cured. This time they tried to overawe him by their authority. They said, "Give glory to God! We ourselves know this Man is a sinner."

The young man met their challenge without fear. He said, "Whether this Man is a sinner, I do not know. One thing I do know, that I was blind and now I see."

His answer surprised and upset them so that for a moment they were speechless and at a loss to know just what to say. They repeated their former question, "What did He do to you? How did He open your eyes?"

The young man felt that the question was useless. He had already told about the cure a number of times. He answered curtly, "I have told you already and you have heard. Would you hear it again?" Then he added scornfully, "Would you also become His disciples?"

This made them furiously angry, for they hated Christ. They said, "We are the disciples of Moses. We know that God spoke to Moses. But for this Man, we do not know where He is from."

The young man was not dismayed. He answered back, "Now this is strange that you do not know where

Jesus, the Good Shepherd

He is from, and yet He opened my eyes. Now we know that God does not hear sinners; but if anyone is a worshiper of God and does His will, him He hears. Not from the beginning of the world has it been heard that anyone opened the eyes of a man born blind. If this Man were not of God He would have no power at all."

By this time the Pharisees were exasperated because they had not been able to silence the man with a satisfactory answer. In their wounded pride they shouted at him, "What! Are we to be taught by you? You were wholly born in sin." And they turned him out; that is, from then on he was not permitted to enter the temple again.

Soon the young man's chastisement was spread abroad and Jesus learned of it. He looked for the man and then with gentle encouragement, by a simple question, tested his faith, "Do you believe in the Son of God?"

His open response showed that he was anxious to know the truth. He asked, "Who is He, Lord, that I may believe in Him?"

And Jesus said, "You have seen Him and It is He Who is speaking with you."

The man, enlightened from above, fell to his knees before Jesus and said, "I believe, Lord."

JESUS, THE GOOD SHEPHERD

John 10:1-18

This Feast of Tabernacles was the last one for Our Lord and therefore, with burning desire He tried to give the people a true picture of His love for them. He spoke of Himself as the "Light of the World" enlightening minds about what is good. Saint John in his Gospel brings out the relation between this idea of Jesus being Light for souls and the miracles worked in favor of the blind man. The man gained not only physical sight, but received a far greater gift, the spiritual sight of the soul. He saw the Light of Faith.

On the last day of the Feast of Tabernacles, Jesus cried out in a loud voice, "If anyone thirst, let him come

The Good Samaritan

to Me and drink. He who believes in Me as the Scripture says, 'From within him there shall flow rivers of living waters.' " With these words Jesus wanted believers to know that the Holy Spirit would live in them.

His words made a deep impression on many who heard Him. Some said, "He is truly a prophet," and others, "this is the Christ, that is, the promised Messias." But not all believed.

About this time, too, He gave a consoling picture of Himself as the Good Shepherd. The Good Shepherd lays down his life for his sheep. But the hireling, he who is not a shepherd, whose own the sheep are not, sees the wolf coming and leaves the sheep and flees. And the wolf catches and scatters the sheep... This idea of a shepherd caring tenderly for his flock was perhaps the clearest way for the people to understand Christ's love and care of them, as they very frequently saw many shepherds with their flocks on the hillsides.

"I am the Good Shepherd, and I know mine and mine know Me, even as the Father knows Me and I know the Father; and I lay down My life for My sheep. And other sheep I have that are not of this fold. Them also I must bring, and they shall hear My voice, and there shall be one fold and one shepherd. For this reason the Father loves Me, because I lay down My life that I may take it up again. No one takes it from Me, but I lay it down of Myself. I have the power to lay it down, and I have the power to take it up again. Such is the command I have received from My Father."

THE GOOD SAMARITAN
Luke 10:29-37

From this story Jesus teaches us that "neighbor" means any man without exception. The scene of the story is a desolate, rocky hill country that lies along the steep incline from Jerusalem to Jericho. If we think about the kind of people Jesus pictured for us we will see deeper meaning in the story. A man is seriously injured and left suffering as two men of his own nation pass by, but later is cared for by a Samaritan. Those who offered no help were really bound by the law of charity, while he who showed charity was considered a hated enemy by those who refused to administer charity.

The parable arose when a Scribe, a Doctor of the Law, asked Our Lord, "Master, what must I do to gain eternal life?"

Jesus replied by putting a question to the Scribe, "What is written in the law? How do you interpret it?"

He answered, "You shall love the Lord your God with your whole heart, and with your whole soul, and with your whole strength, and with your whole mind; and your neighbor as yourself."

Jesus approved what he said and replied, "You have answered rightly; do this and you shall live."

The Scribe was not satisfied. He questioned further, "And who is my neighbor?"

And then Jesus told the story of the good Samaritan: "A certain man was going down from Jerusalem to Jericho, and he fell in with robbers, who after both stripping and beating him went their way, leaving him half dead. But, as it happened, a certain priest was going down the same way, and when he saw him, passed by. And likewise a Levite also, and when he was near the place and saw him, passed by. But a certain Samaritan as he journeyed, came upon him, and seeing him, was moved to compassion. And he went up to him and bound up his wounds, pouring in oil and wine. And setting him on his own beast, he brought him to an inn and took care of him. And the next day he took out two denarii and gave them to the innkeeper and said, 'Take care of him; and whatever more you spend, I, on my way back, will repay you.' "

Our Lord then asked the question: "Which of these three, in your opinion, was neighbor to him who fell among robbers?"

The Scribe had no choice but to reply, "He who took pity on him."

Jesus answered gravely, "Go and do you also in like manner."

Luke 10:38-42

After Our Lord had finished the story about the Good Samaritan, He and His apostles continued their walk along the dangerous road from Jerusalem to Jericho. About half-way along the main road, a side road branched south to Bethany. The whole party took this road. Jesus was on His way to the house of His friends, Lazarus and Martha and Mary. It was a stopping-place familiar to the apostles; they were always welcome there.

By mid-morning they reached a comfortable home built against wooded hills. After a hearty welcome, the company settled down in the sunny courtyard near the entrance to the house. Martha stepped into the house, full of interest in preparing a meal for the guests. As Martha started her work, she realized that Mary had not come in to help her. She waited and yet Mary did not come. Somewhat anxious about getting everything in readiness, she went out to look for Mary. Surprised, she saw Mary sitting at the feet of Jesus, intent on every word He said. Mary did not even notice Martha was looking for her.

Martha, politely, but yet somewhat peevishly, addressed herself to Jesus, "Lord, is it no concern of Yours that my sister has left me alone to serve? Tell her to help me."

Mary remained silent and looked at Jesus, wondering if He would tell her to leave.

Jesus answered Martha affectionately but with some seriousness, "Martha, Martha, you are anxious and troubled about many things; and yet, but one thing is necessary." Then pointing to her sister Mary, He continued, "Mary has chosen the best part and it will not be taken away from her."

Jesus spoke in Mary's defense and admonished Martha. Mary, in listening to the words of Jesus and putting all else out of her mind, was doing a better thing than Martha. Martha on the other hand was doing a

Martha and Mary

very necessary work, and Jesus did not tell her to stop her work and sit down and listen to Him.

In speaking to these two sisters as He did, Jesus wants us to understand that in life there are times when we should do nothing but listen and think about the word of God; and at other times we should do the things that must be done. The first is the better thing to do and the more important one; the second is necessary and must be attended to.

After Christ's gentle admonition Martha returned to her work without annoyance about Mary. And Jesus later enjoyed and was grateful for the services of Martha.

THE OUR FATHER

Luke 11:1-4

Saint Luke tells us about an occasion when the disciples had an opportunity to see Jesus absorbed in prayer. It impressed them so that when He had finished praying they said to Him, "Lord, teach us to pray."

Our Lord was pleased at their request and said to them: "When you pray say, 'Our Father Who art in heaven, hallowed be Thy name. Thy kingdom come, Thy will be done on earth, as it is in heaven. Give us this day our daily bread, and forgive us our trespasses, as we forgive those who trespass against us. And lead us not into temptation, but deliver us from evil.' "

After Jesus said this prayer for the people He told two stories to help them understand that there is more to prayer than just words. He told them about a man who was very much in need of bread. It was already night, but he had to have the bread immediately. Now he went to his friend's house to borrow the bread but his friend and all his family had already gone to bed and the door was locked. At the first knock on his friend's door, the man refused to get up, but after several knocks he did get up, opened the door and handed bread to the waiting man. That is the way it is with prayer. If at first

The Our Father

your request is not granted, continue to pray. Never give up. This is called the spirit of perseverance in prayer.

Then Jesus told a second story to show that when we pray to Our Father in heaven, we should keep in mind that He is a Father and the best of all fathers. "If a child asks bread of his father," Jesus said, "would the father give his child a stone?" And then with much tenderness He added, "If fathers here on earth give good gifts to their children, will not your Father in heaven give you all those things that are good for you?"

In many instances Holy Scripture shows Our Lord at prayer and it also repeats valuable instructions about prayer that He gave to His disciples. The humble prayer of the publican, "O Lord, be merciful to me a sinner" was heard, but the prayer of the proud Pharisee was not acceptable. All the appeals to Our Lord for cures were heard when they were made in the spirit of faith and humility. We read that Our Lord frequently spent the whole night in prayer. He prayed in His hour of agony. He prayed on the cross. His prayer to His heavenly Father at the Last Supper was a most touching appeal of loving trust. "Prayer," the right kind of prayer, as the Scripture says, "can move mountains."

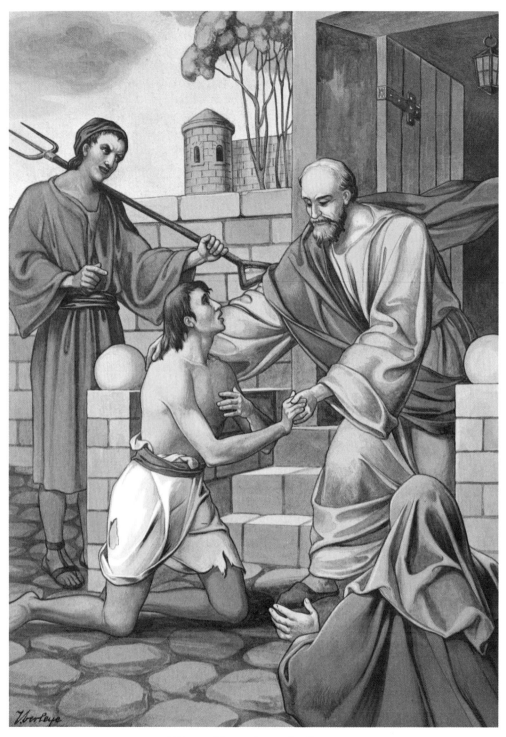

The Prodigal Son

Luke 15:11-32

No story told by Christ shows so truly His great love for sinners as that of this wasteful son.

A man had two sons. The younger said to his father, "Sir, give me my inheritance." Having received it, he left home and went into a far country where he spent all he had in riotous living. And then a famine came into that land. In a short time he was reduced to complete poverty. He found work as a keeper of pigs.

Lonesome and hungry, he thought within himself, "The many servants in my father's house have more bread than they can eat and here I am perishing with hunger. I will arise and go to my father and say to him, 'Father, I have sinned against heaven and you. I am not worthy now to be called your son. Treat me as one of your hired servants.' "

He arose and started for home. But while he was still a far way off, his father saw him. Running to meet him, he threw his arms about him and kissed him. And then the son said, "Father, I am not worthy to be called your son." The father would not listen. He called to his servants, "Bring out the best robes, put a ring on his hand and shoes on his feet. Prepare a feast. Let us eat and make merry, for my son here, was dead and has come back to life again. He was lost and is found." And the merrymaking began.

The elder son had been away. As he drew near the house he heard the merrymaking. On learning the reason for it, he refused to go into the house. His father tried to win him over but his son said, "I have lived as your son and have never transgressed your commands but you have never made me a present of even a young goat to make merry with my friends; and now when this son of yours who has squandered your wealth in fast living comes home, you have killed the fatted calf in his honor."

He said to him, "My son, you are always at my side, and everything I have is yours; but for this rejoicing and merrymaking there was good reason; your brother was dead and has come back to life again; was lost and is found."

245

The Ten Lepers

Luke 17:11-19

Because of their terrible and contagious disease, lepers, in the time of Our Lord, were required by law to live apart and never appear in public. So they had to leave their families, wear a special dress, and live in places away from cities and towns. Their lot was a most wretched one.

Jesus at this time was on His way to Jerusalem and was passing between Samaria and Galilee. As He entered a nearby town, ten men who were lepers saw Him in the distance. They kept far away as the law prescribed, but they shouted to Jesus, saying, "Jesus, Master, have mercy on us."

Their cry touched Jesus and He said to them, "Go, show yourselves to the priests."

Now anyone who claimed to be cured from leprosy was obliged to go before the priests, whose duty it was to examine such claims and approve the cure. Only then could lepers return to their homes and take their place in public again.

The cure of these ten men did not take place immediately, as had happened to all other lepers Jesus had cured. Jesus required more faith from these. Although they were still filled with leprosy when they started out to show themselves to the priests, they trusted in the command they had received, and as they went on their way, the leprosy left them.

The ending of this wonderful story, however, is not a pleasant one. We would expect that after such a miracle all who were cured would have returned to give thanks to their Benefactor. But only one returned and he was a Samaritan, one of that group hated by the Jews. The Gospel story leads one to believe that the other nine were Jews. Jesus felt what ingratitude was like, for when the Samaritan, deeply grateful, threw himself at the feet of Jesus with his face to the ground, Jesus said, "Were not ten made clean? And where are the nine? There is no one found to return and give glory to God but this stranger." Turning to the Samaritan, Jesus said, "Arise, go your way; your faith has cured you."

The Pharisee and the Publican

THE PHARISEE AND THE PUBLICAN

Luke 18:9-14

Again Jesus speaks to the people about prayer. He tells them about two men who came to the temple to pray. We will understand the story much better if we first learn about the two men who take part in the interesting story. One was a Pharisee. He was one of a group of people, Jews, who thought themselves to be much more religious-minded than even other Jews, and in his prayer and in his life he acted as if he did not need God's help. His prayer was detestable before God because he had a proud heart. The other man was a publican. Publicans were Jews also, but they were thought of as unfaithful, unjust and sinners because they collected taxes from the people for the hated Romans.

The parable is this: "Two men went up into the temple to pray: the one a Pharisee and the other a publican. The Pharisee standing, prayed thus within himself, 'O God, I give You thanks that I am not as the rest of men, extortioners, unjust, adulterers as also is this publican. I fast twice a week; I give away one-tenth of all I possess.' And the publican, standing afar off, would not so much as lift up his eyes toward heaven but struck his breast, crying, 'O God, be merciful to me, a sinner!'" Jesus concluded the parable in these words: "I say to you, this man went down into his house justified, that is, pleasing to God, rather than the other because every one that exalts himself shall be humbled and he that humbles himself shall be exalted."

Christ Blesses Little Children

Luke 18:15-17

There were two occasions when Jesus showed how much He loved little children.

At one time the apostles were traveling in groups along the road to Capharnaum to Peter's house. Jesus waited until all had arrived and then asked them, "What were you talking of on the way?"

The apostles were embarrassed, because they had been disputing which of them should be the greatest. But Jesus, knowing why they did not want to answer, did not demand a reply. Instead, He called a child that was near and drew the little one to Himself. The apostles looked at each other in surprise, wondering what the Master was going to do. Then Jesus called the apostles in a circle around Him and said to them, "Amen I say to you, unless you change your ways and become as little children, you shall not enter the kingdom of heaven." And he added, "Whosoever, therefore, shall humble himself as this little child, he is the greater in the kingdom of heaven. And he that shall receive one such little child in My name receives Me."

One day sometime later, Jesus had spoken at some length to a group of women and now when He had finished the sun was already beginning to set and He was tired. While the crowd began to move away, some women with babies in their arms timidly approached Jesus. They asked Him to lay His hands in blessing on their little ones. Seeing that Jesus was pleased at the request, other mothers followed and then a number of children took courage, too, and ran to Jesus.

The apostles did not like it. Their Master was tired and besides, it was just a waste of their Master's time to have little ones come to Him like this. They made signs for everybody to move on.

But Jesus rebuked His apostles and motioned the mothers and the children to come. He said, "Let the little children come to Me, and forbid them not for of such is the kingdom of heaven."

The Rich Young Man

THE RICH YOUNG MAN

Luke 18:18-30

After Jesus had finished blessing the little ones, He made ready to leave, in order to continue His journey south. A young man ran up to Him, knelt down before Him and asked, "Good Master, what must I do to obtain eternal life?"

And Jesus said to him, "If you wish eternal life, keep the commandments."

The young man asked, "Which commandments?"

Jesus answered, "You shall not murder, you shall not commit adultery, you shall not steal, you shall not bear false witness, you shall not wrong any man, honor your father and your mother, and you shall love your neighbor as yourself."

The young man replied, "All these I have observed since my youth, what is still wanting to me?"

Then Jesus looked at him and loved him and said, "In one thing you are still wanting. If you wish to be perfect, go home and sell all you have and give it to the poor, and so you shall have treasure in heaven; then come and follow Me." To this the young man said nothing but he went away sorrowing, for he had great treasures.

And Jesus looked around and said to the disciples, "With what difficulty will those who have riches enter God's kingdom! It is easier for a camel to pass through the eye of a needle than for a rich man to enter the kingdom of heaven."

His disciples wondered. They said among themselves, "Who then can be saved?" Jesus looked at them and answered, "Such things are impossible to man's power, but not to God's. To God all things are possible."

Then Peter said to Jesus, "We have left all things to follow You, what will we receive?"

Jesus then said to His disciples, "Amen I say to you: there is no man who has left house or brother or sister or father or mother or children for My sake or the Gospel who will not receive, now in this world, a hundred times as much in houses, brothers, sisters, mothers, children and lands, but with persecution. And in the world to come, he will receive life everlasting. But many will be first that were last, and last, that were first."

The Raising of Lazarus from the Grave

John 11:1-44

Lazarus of Bethany had fallen sick. His sisters Martha and Mary, seeing that their brother's illness was growing worse, sent a message to Jesus, their friend, saying, "Lord, behold, he whom You love is sick."

Hearing it Jesus said, "This sickness is not unto death, but for the glory of God; that the Son of God may be glorified by it." Although Jesus loved Martha and Mary, He still remained two days longer in Perea. After that time He said to the apostles, "Let us go again to Judea."

The disciples remembered that at their last visit they had to leave Jerusalem for fear of being stoned. They said, "Rabbi, just now the Jews were seeking to stone You; and are You going there again?"

Jesus quieted their fears by telling them that nothing happens unless it be God's will. Then He told them the reason for the journey, "Lazarus, our friend, sleeps, but I go to awake him from his sleep."

The disciples not anxious to go said, "Lord, if he sleeps it is well." They thought of sleep as a sign of physical improvement.

Then Jesus said to them plainly, "Lazarus is dead; and I rejoice on your account that I was not there that you may believe. But let us go to him."

The disciples made ready to follow Jesus but their hearts were disturbed. Thomas tried to cover his fears and theirs by saying, with an attempt at courage, "Let us also go, that we may die with Him."

So, on the fourth day after having received the message, they set out for Bethany. Bethany was but a short distance from Jerusalem and many relatives and friends had come to Bethany to comfort Martha and Mary. Martha, when she heard that Jesus was coming, went out to meet Him, while Mary remained at home. Throwing herself at Our Lord's feet, Martha said, "Lord, if You had been here, my brother would not have died." And then hinting timidly, she showed her great expectation of seeing her brother again by saying simply, "But even now I know that whatever You ask of God, God will give it to You."

Jesus said simply, "Your brother will rise again."

Martha said to Him, "I know he will rise again at the resurrection, when the last day comes."

Then in a solemn manner Jesus said some very beautiful words, "I am the resurrection and the life; he who believes in Me, even if he dies, shall live; and whoever lives and believes in Me, shall never die. Do you believe this?"

With sincere faith Martha replied, "Yes, Lord, I believe that You are the Christ, the Son of God, Who has come into the world."

With this, Martha went to call her sister Mary who was in the midst of relatives and friends. Martha whispered to her, "The Master is here and bids you come." Swiftly Mary ran to Him, and throwing herself on her knees, weeping, repeated the words Martha had said, "Lord, if You had been here my brother would not have died."

The Jews who were in the house with Mary comforting her, when they saw her rise speedily and run toward the tomb, went out to follow her, saying, "She has gone to weep."

Seeing Mary and her companions in tears, Jesus sighed deeply and was troubled in spirit. He said, "Where have you laid him?" They said to Him, "Come and see." And Jesus wept.

When those present saw Jesus weep, they said, "See how He loved him." But not all were moved by Our Lord's tears. Some said, "Could not He who opened the eyes of the man born blind, have caused that this man should not die?"

Jesus again gave a deep sigh as He came to the tomb. It was a cave, and a stone was laid over it. "Take the stone away," Jesus commanded.

Martha, Lazarus' sister, objected. She said, "Lord, by this time he is already decayed, for he is dead four days."

With a slight reproach in His voice, Jesus said to Martha, "Have I not told you that if you believe, you shall behold the glory of God?"

Then lifting His eyes toward heaven He prayed, "Father I thank You for hearing My prayer. For myself, I know that You hear Me at all times, but I say this for the people that are standing around, that they may learn to believe it is You who have sent Me." When He said this He cried out with a loud voice, "Lazarus, come forth!" And at once he who had been dead came forth, bound hands and feet, and his face bound about with the wrappings of death. Jesus said to them, "Loose him, and let him go."

Many who had seen this great marvel believed in Jesus, but some of them went to the Pharisees and told them the things that Jesus had done. The Pharisees and the priests were alarmed and called a council and said, "What shall we do for this Man is performing many miracles? If we let Him alone all will believe in Him and the Romans will come and take away our city and our nation."

Caiphas, the high priest, cut their argument short. He said, "You know nothing at all, nor do you realize that it is for the good of our nation that one Man die instead of the whole nation perishing." So from that day on, the matter was decided—Jesus would die. It was only for them to choose a suitable time and make at least some sort of pretense of following the necessary steps of the law.

Zacchaeus

Jericho was an important commercial city where there was need for many tax gatherers. These men were not liked by the townsfolk because they collected the tribute money imposed upon the Jews by their conquerors, the Romans. The tax gatherers were Jews, but they were considered sinners and renegades and were known by the hated title "publican". Zacchaeus was a leading publican, rich, but despised.

One day when he heard that Jesus was entering Jericho, he hastened toward the crowd that was gathering to see Him. He wanted to get a glimpse of this Man of Whom he had heard so much. But Zacchaeus was not a tall man and could not see because of the crowd. So he ran on ahead of the crowd and climbed into a sycamore tree. When Our Lord, surrounded by the multitude, came under the tree, He looked up and said, "Zacchaeus, make haste and come down; for this day I must abide in your house."

He was startled to hear Jesus call his name! He came down immediately and with great joy made Jesus welcome at his home.

The crowd indeed wondered that Jesus should enter the house of a tax gatherer, especially that belonging to Zacchaeus. They openly complained saying, "He has gone to be the guest of a man who is a sinner."

Jesus paid no attention to the complaining crowd. He had come to save sinners and in His eyes Zacchaeus was ready for conversion; he was ready to come back to the fold.

Zacchaeus surprised and silenced the complainers. Standing, he said to the Lord, "Behold, I give one-half of my possessions to the poor, and if I have wronged anyone in any way I restore him fourfold."

Moved by the publican's good will, Jesus turned and exclaimed, "Today salvation has come to this house, because he, too, is a son of Abraham, for the Son of Man came to seek and to save what is lost."

Mary Anoints the Feet of Jesus

John 12:1-8

Six days before the Paschal feast Jesus went to Bethany to the home of Lazarus whom He had raised from the dead. On the evening of the following day, which was the Sabbath, Simon, a wealthy man, and formerly a leper, had planned a supper for Jesus to which Lazarus and the apostles were invited. Martha, the sister of Lazarus, served. When they were seated at table Mary came in carrying a box of spikenard, a costly perfume. Kneeling at the feet of Jesus, she broke the alabaster vase, a delicate white-stone jar, and anointed His feet and wiped them with her hair. The whole house was fragrant with the odor of it.

The disciples, when they saw the waste, were indignant and said among themselves, "Why all this waste?"

One of the disciples, Judas Iscariot, he who was about to betray Jesus, said, "Why was not this ointment sold for three hundred pence and given to the poor?" Judas did not really care for the poor. He said this because he was a thief and since he was charged with taking care of the money belonging to the disciples, the money received for the perfume would have gone through his hands and he could have kept it.

Jesus came to the defense of Mary, saying, "Why do you trouble this woman? She has done Me a good turn, for the poor you have always with you, but you will not always have Me. She has done what she could. She has anointed My body beforehand to prepare it for burial. Amen I say to you, wherever in the whole world this Gospel is preached, this also that she has done shall be told in memory of her."

The Triumphal Entry into Jerusalem

John 12:12-19

Hundreds of years before Our Lord's entry into Jerusalem, a great prophet, Ezechiel, through an inspiration from God, foretold the things that were going to happen at the entry of Jesus into Jerusalem. He said it would be an occasion of jubilation and triumph and he told it in these words: "Rejoice greatly, O daughter of Sion! Shout for joy, O daughter of Jerusalem! Behold your King will come to you, the Just, the Savior. He is poor and sitting upon an ass, and upon a colt, the foal of an ass."

On this first Palm Sunday, in the city of Jerusalem, Our Lord was going to fulfill the prophecy, or in other words, do what the prophet said would happen. All good Jewish people knew the prophecy and when they saw Jesus riding into Jerusalem as He did, they knew without any doubt that He was proclaiming Himself the Messias, the Son of God, their King.

The week of the Pasch was always a tremendous time in Jerusalem. The Roman authorities were especially alert that no insurrection would occur. The Pharisees and the priests, too, were vigilant, but this year there was added strain and anxiety. They had certain knowledge that Jesus would be in Jerusalem for the celebration and since the decision had been made to kill Him, they had somehow to trap Him and yet avoid a tumult among the people.

In the mind of Christ this Palm Sunday was the day set for His triumphal entry into Jerusalem. Before this, on several occasions Jesus fled from the midst of the people when they wanted to make Him king. But on this day, to the surprise of all, He encouraged their enthusiasm. He knew His hour was come. He would make His last claim to be the Messias. Without a word of direction He controlled the procession even into Jerusalem itself and into the temple. He chose the time—the week during which Jerusalem was crowded with visitors and it was also the week during which He would die. He chose the place—on the road from Bethany over Mount Olivet, into the Holy City and into the temple. He chose the manner in which He would appear—as the Royal Heir of the House of David, yet riding humbly on an ass. He appeared as a poor King with no earthly kingdom. Although the event was public, glorious and triumphant, neither the Romans nor His bitter enemies dared to interfere.

A great number of visitors in Jerusalem had heard that Jesus was in Bethany and they made the trip there to see Him. They also hoped to see Lazarus, the man that had been dead in the tomb for four days. All these people and many, too, from Bethany itself, planned to go up to Jerusalem when Jesus was ready to go.

The procession started out from Bethany and the crowd, in a happy mood, picked palm branches and waved them, singing as they went. To their surprise, Jesus did not stop them. When they were nearing Bethphage, Jesus said to two disciples, "Go to the village that faces you, and on entering it, you will find the colt of an ass tied, on which no man has ridden. Loose him and bring him to Me. If any man shall ask you, 'Why do you loose him?' you shall say to him, 'The Lord has need of him.'" And they brought the colt to Jesus.

The disciples laid their garments on the colt and Jesus sat on him. The crowd went wild with excitement when they saw Jesus riding as He was. Ezechiel's prophetic words were in every mind. He was their King. He was about to enter His kingdom. By this time other groups from neighboring towns came out from Jerusalem to give honor to Christ, the Son of God. Cloaks were strewn in the way, branches of palms and olive trees were cut and waved. The air was rent with shouts and acclamations, "Hosanna in the highest." By the time the jubilant crowd had reached the summit of Mount Olivet, the Pharisees already had word that Jesus was about to enter Jerusalem, acclaimed King by the populace. In haste they came upon the procession and going up to Jesus in angry tones shouted above the lusty cheers, "Master, rebuke Your disciples."

Jesus looked at them and with great firmness replied, "I tell you that if these keep silence, the stones will cry out."

The procession moved on until it reached a point from which the city of Jerusalem lay before the eyes of

Jesus in the glorious splendor of the setting sun. He stopped and looked at it. Then He wept and made a woeful prophecy: "If you had known in this your day, even you, the things that are for your peace! But now they are hidden from your eyes. For days will come upon you when your enemies will throw a rampart about you and surround you and shut you in on every side, and will dash you to the ground and your children within you. They will not leave within you one stone upon another because you have not known the time of your visitation." It was a fearful prediction of things to come.

But the crowd was too hopeful and joyous to notice any delay and few heard the awful words. Soon the procession moved into the city where all were stirred at the unusual sight. "Who is this?" they asked.

The crowd answered, "This is Jesus, the Prophet of Nazareth, in Galilee."

When Jesus came into the temple men who were blind and lame came up to Him and He healed them. The children in the temple, taking up the refrain from the crowd, also cried, "Hosanna to the Son of David." The Pharisees tried to quiet them and in their wrath, said to Jesus, "Do You hear what they are saying?"

"Yes," Jesus answered. "Have you never read these words, 'Out of the mouths of infants and sucklings you have perfected praise?' "

Knowing that at the moment nothing could be done they walked away muttering each to the other, "Do you see that nobody pays any attention to us? Behold, the whole world has gone after Him!"

And leaving Jerusalem, Jesus and the twelve went into Bethany and remained there.

THE BETRAYAL

Matthew 26:14-16

Judas had been with Jesus during the entire public ministry, but all through this time of instruction and enlightenment he did not look for the good he might learn to do for others. Judas was selfish. He loved money and hoped that in the service of the Messias he might secure a position of importance. As

The Washing of the Feet

Christ's teaching unfolded and the spirit of His charity, His humility, His love for the poor showed themselves, Judas became more and more dissatisfied. And when of late Jesus had spoken so plainly of what was to come, Judas decided that a change soon would be best.

An opportunity to get away from it all came. It was immediately after the supper at Bethany when Judas had been angered at Christ's praise of the waste, as he had considered it.

In some way Judas learned that the chief priests were to hold a special council concerning the need to do away with Christ. They were of a mind to get rid of Him quickly, even before the festival, but hesitated to seize Him publicly. And then Judas came, one of the twelve, to bargain with them. It was an unhoped for opportunity. He promised to deliver Jesus to them secretly as soon as there was a chance. This was just what they had been looking for. They offered him thirty pieces of silver for his sacrilegious treachery and the bargain was settled. Judas went back to Christ and the apostles.

THE WASHING OF THE FEET

John 13:1-17

On Thursday of the same week the disciples asked Jesus, "Where do you want us to prepare for the Passover?"

In answer Jesus selected two of the apostles, Peter and John, and gave them this instruction: "Go into the city and there you will meet a man carrying a pitcher of water; follow him. Wherever he enters, say to the master of the house, 'The Master says, "Where is My guest chamber that I may eat the Passover there with My disciples?"' And he will show you a large upper room furnished, and there make ready for us." Everything happened as Jesus had foretold.

And when evening had come Jesus sat at table with His twelve apostles. Jesus knew that His hour was near at hand, that He was soon to pass out of this world to the Father. He loved His apostles and wanted to give them proof of His love. He said to them, "I have greatly desired to eat this Passover with you before I suffer."

Then Jesus took a bowl of wine which was prescribed by Law as the opening ceremony of the Passover, blessed it and said, "Take this and share it among you." As the supper had thus begun and conversation started, a dispute arose among the apostles as to who would be the greater. Jesus offered no word of correction, but in a way that they would never forget, He showed them how they should act one toward the other. They were to be as servants, being helpful and not having rivalries among themselves.

Jesus rose from the table, laid aside His outer garment and taking a towel, girded Himself with it and put water into a basin. As Jesus made these preparations discussion stopped and all eyes were upon Him. They did not know what He was planning to do. And then, basin in hand, He went up to Peter's couch and knelt, ready to wash his feet. Peter was struck with amazement that the Master should wash his feet. He said, "Lord, are You going to wash my feet?"

Our Lord answered, "It is not for you to know now what I am doing, but you will understand it hereafter."

Peter said, drawing back, "I will never let You wash my feet."

"If I do not wash you," was the positive reply, "you will have no companionship with Me."

No part with Christ? That would never do! With great ardor Peter quickly replied, "Not my feet only, but also my hands and my head!"

Jesus answered, "He who has bathed needs only to wash, and he is clean all over. And you are clean, but not all." Jesus said these words because of Judas. But Judas was hardened in his sin. There was no sorrow in his heart.

After Jesus had finished washing the feet of all of the disciples and those of Judas, too, He put on His outer garment again and sat at table. Looking with affection at His twelve, He said to them: "Do you know what I have done to you? You call Me Master and Lord and you say well, for so I am. If, therefore, I, your Lord and Master, have washed your feet, you also ought to wash the feet of one another. For I have given you an example, that as I have done to you, so you should do also."

Jesus continued to speak and brought out very pointedly the cause of the sorrow that was in His Heart, the unfaithfulness of one of His own twelve. He said further, "If you know the things I have taught you, blessed shall you be if you do them. I do not speak of you all..."

And then solemnly and troubled in spirit He said to all at table, "Amen, Amen, I say to you, one of you will betray Me."

The quiet words aroused great confusion in the minds and hearts of His devoted disciples. They looked at each other, wondering who among them could be guilty. The thought of such a crime horrified them. Then the question, "Is it I, Lord?" went from lip to lip, and even Judas dared to ask the question. Jesus answered him in a whisper, "You have said it." Judas was seated near Our Lord and in the confusion of the moment, no one heard what Jesus had said.

After the immediate excitement had lessened, Peter's desire to know who the traitor was, left him no peace. He told John to ask Jesus who it was. In a low tone John said, "Lord, who is it?"

Jesus answered, "It is he for whom I shall dip the bread, and give it to him." Jesus moistened a piece of bread and gave it to Judas. In doing this Jesus gave Judas another opportunity to express sorrow, but he did not. He refused this special grace and the Gospel adds "After the morsel, Satan entered into him."

And Jesus said to Judas, "What you are going to do, do quickly."

Saint John finished the story, "But none of those at the table understood why He said this to him. For some thought that because Judas held the purse Jesus said to him, 'Buy the things we need for the feast;' or that he should give something to the poor. When, therefore, he had received the morsel he went out quickly. Now it was night."

THE LAST SUPPER

Matthew 26:26-35

When Judas had gone out of the Cenacle a great burden seemed lifted from the Heart of Jesus. He spoke of the great glory that was to come. His bitter passion would glorify the Father and redeem mankind, and the Father would glorify Him in the Resurrection and the Ascension, which were to follow the sufferings of Good Friday. The justice, the goodness and the mercy of the Father would be made known.

And now the time had come to fulfill the great promise Jesus had made at Capharnaum. He would give them His flesh to eat and His blood to drink.

"And while they were still at table, Jesus took bread, and blessed it and broke it, and gave it to His apostles, saying, 'Take and eat; this is My body which is given for you. Do this in commemoration of Me.' And taking the cup, He gave thanks and gave it to them, saying, 'All of you drink of this, for this is My blood of the New Testament which is being shed for many unto the forgiveness of sins.'"

After they had received Holy Communion, Jesus spoke to them. His Heart was full of love and anxiety. He called them "little children". He said, "Little children, yet a little while I am with you. You will seek Me but where I go you cannot come." And then they heard Christ's great commandment of love: "A new commandment I give you; that you love one another; that as I have loved you, you also love one another. By this shall all men know that you are My disciples, if you love one another."

It bothered Peter that Jesus said He was going where they could not come. He asked, "Lord, where are You going?"

"Where I am going," Jesus answered, "you cannot follow Me now, but you will follow Me later."

Peter did not want to wait. He wanted to go now. "Why cannot I follow now? I will lay down my life for You."

The Last Supper

Peter meant what he said and loved Jesus enough to lay down his life for Him but Peter was not yet strong enough in the spirit. Jesus knew what would happen within a few hours. He said, "You will lay down your life for Me? Amen, Amen, I say to you, the cock will not crow before you have denied Me three times." And then Jesus added, "Simon, Simon, behold Satan has desired to have you, that he may sift you as wheat, but I have prayed for you that your faith may not fail; and do you, when once you have been strengthened, help your brothers."

Peter felt sure that he would never deny his Lord and he insisted, "Lord, I am ready to go with You to prison and to death."

Jesus did not argue with Peter but told him again more forcibly, "I tell you, Peter, a cock will not crow this day, until you have denied three times that you know Me."

The foretelling of Peter's denial made all the other apostles fearful of what they themselves might do. Our Lord tried to calm their fears and to strengthen them to bear sufferings. "Let not your heart be troubled," He said, "You believe also in Me. In My Father's house there are many mansions. Were it not so I would have told you, because I go to prepare a place for you. And if I go and prepare a place for you, I am coming again, and I will take you to Myself; that where I am, there you also may be. And where I go you know, and the way you know."

Thomas interrupted, "Lord, we do not know where You are going, and how can we know the way?"

The words that Jesus gave in answer to Thomas' question, point the way to heaven for every soul. With a majesty which belongs to God alone, Jesus answered most solemnly, "I am the Way, the Truth and the Life. No one comes to the Father but through Me. If you had known Me, you would also have known My Father. You do know Him, and you have seen Him."

And when Jesus had finished speaking Philip asked, "Lord, show us the Father and it is enough for us."

Jesus' answer was a mild reproof. "Have I been so long a time with you, and you have not known Me? Philip, he who sees Me sees also the Father and the Father in Me. How can you say, 'Show us the Father?' Do you not believe that I am in the Father and the Father is in Me? The words that I speak to you I speak not of My own authority. But the Father dwelling in Me, it is He Who does the works I do. Do you believe that I am in the Father and the Father is in Me? Otherwise, believe because of the works themselves."

The apostles were slow to understand all Jesus was trying to teach them. They should have known the close relation that existed between Jesus and the Father. Yet He explained it again with very great patience. He told them of the perfect unity that exists between God the Father and Himself, the Son. Both have the same Divine Nature. Knowing the Son then, meant that they know the Father also.

"If you have any love for Me, you must keep the Commandments which I gave you; and then I will ask the Father, and He will give you Another to befriend you, One Who is to dwell continually with you forever. It is the truth-giving Spirit, for Whom the world can find no room, because it cannot see Him, cannot recognize Him. But you are to recognize Him; He will be continually at your side, nay, He will be in you."

And He added, "This Holy Spirit will teach you all things, and bring to your mind whatever I have said to you."

"Peace I leave you, My peace I give to you; not as the world gives do I give to you. Do not let your heart be troubled, or afraid."

All Israel was familiar with the growth and care of the vine. Our Lord compared Himself to a vine and those who follow Him, to its branches, and His Father is the vine dresser. He cuts and takes care of the vine. He trims the branches so they will bear more fruit. Those that yield no fruit He cuts off and throws them into the fire.

To His apostles Jesus said, "I am the true vine, and My Father is the vine dresser. Every branch in Me that bears no fruit He will take away; and every branch that bears fruit He will cleanse, that it may bear more fruit... As a branch cannot bear fruit of itself unless it remain in the vine, so neither can you unless you abide in Me. He who abides in Me and I in him bears much fruit; for without Me you can do nothing."

On this night, again and again, Jesus stressed the observance of the Commandments. Jesus finished the lesson on the vine by saying, "If you keep My Commandments you will abide in My love... These things I have spoken to you that My joy may be in you, and that your joy may be full."

There are ten Commandments and then there is the Great Commandment of love. Christ tells us that all the Commandments are included in the Great Commandment and He calls it My Commandment: "This is My Commandment that you love one another as I have loved you. Greater love than this no one has, that one lay down his life for his friends. You are My friends, if you do the things I command you. No longer do I call you servants, because the servant does not know what his master does. But I call you friends, because all the things that I have heard from My Father I have made known to you... These things I command you, that you may love one another."

Our Lord knew His apostles would suffer because they were to teach the things He taught. They needed divine light and strength to carry on Christ's teaching, which is the only way to heaven. Satan and the wicked on earth would do all they possibly could to stop the work of the apostles but nevertheless, the work of the Holy Spirit would go on.

Sorrow filled the hearts of the apostles because Jesus had told them what to expect after He had gone, but He told them He was speaking the truth in telling them that it is better that He go. Then He said, "But if I go I will send an Advocate. He is the Spirit of truth. The Holy Spirit will teach the world about the Father. Many things yet I have to say to you, but you cannot bear them now. But when He, the Spirit of truth has come, He will teach you all truth."

The time for the departure was nearing. The apostles were bewildered about all these things and then Jesus, to give them assurance said, "Amen, Amen I say to you that you shall weep and lament, but the world shall rejoice; and you shall be sorrowful, but your sorrow shall be turned to joy. You shall have sorrow now; but I will see you again, and your heart shall rejoice, and your joy no one shall take from you... Take courage, I have overcome the world."

Then they all stood and sang the final hymn, after which Our Lord raised His eyes to heaven and prayed to His eternal Father. He had been speaking about His Father. Now, in His last moments with His apostles, He speaks to His Father. As He prays, the apostles can see and hear how close is the union between Jesus and the Father.

The first prayer to the Father is for Himself. He says, "Father, the time has come; give glory now to Your Son that the Son may give glory to You."

But most of His prayer is for those who are going to do His work on earth after He is gone, His apostles: "I have made Your name known to the men (apostles) whom You have entrusted to Me, chosen out of the world... Holy Father, keep them true to Your name that they may be one, as We are one. As long as I was with them, it was for Me to keep them true to Your name; and I have watched over them, so that only one has been lost... But now I am coming to You; and while I am still in the world I am telling them these things, so that My joy may be theirs, and may reach full measure in them. I have given them Your message, and the world has nothing but hatred for them, because they do not belong to the world, as I, too, do not belong to the world. I am not asking that You should take them out of the world, but that You should keep them clear of what is evil. Keep them holy then, through the truth; it is Your word that is truth. You have sent Me into the world on your errand, and I have sent them into the world on My errand; and I dedicate Myself for their sakes, that they, too, may be dedicated through the truth."

In the last part of the prayer Jesus prays for all who through the centuries will believe in Him: "It is not only for them that I pray; I pray for those who are to find faith in Me through their word; that they all may be one; that they too may be in Us, as You, Father, are in Me, and I in You; so that the world may come to believe that it is You Who have sent Me... Father, You are just; the world has never acknowledged You, but I have acknowledged You, and these men have acknowledged that You sent Me. I have revealed and will reveal Your Name to them; so that the love You have bestowed upon Me may dwell in them, and I, too, may dwell in them."

THE AGONY IN THE GARDEN

Matthew 26:36-46

When Jesus and the apostles left the upper room, darkness had fallen over Jerusalem, but the full moon shone brightly, lighting up the valley before them. They passed through the gate in the city wall, went down a steep incline and at the bottom, crossed the brook of Cedron by a small bridge.

On the other side of the brook, a little distance up the path, was the Garden of Gethsemani. At its entrance Jesus stopped and told eight of His eleven apostles to wait at the gate. He warned them to pray, that they might not fall into temptation. Then taking Peter and James and John with Him, He went a little farther and now Jesus grew sad and afraid. "My soul," He said to them, "is ready to die with sorrow. Stay here and pray and watch with Me."

Jesus then left the apostles and walked about a stone's throw further into the garden. There, alone, in the darkness of the night He knelt. And then, with His forehead pressed to the earth He cried in anguish,

The Agony in the Garden

"Father, if it be possible, let this chalice pass away from Me; yet not as I will, but as You will." The sufferings which Jesus was to endure were more than an ordinary man could bear. Even in this awful moment He wanted above all things to do His Father's will; but the nearness and the reality of every detail of suffering brought this cry of anguish from His lips.

When He rose from prayer, He returned to the three apostles. He was pained to see that they had fallen asleep. "Simon, how can you sleep?" He asked sadly. "Can you not watch an hour with Me? Watch and pray lest you enter into temptation. The spirit indeed is willing but the flesh is weak."

Then He went back again and prayed a second time. Again He spoke to His heavenly Father, "My Father, if this chalice cannot pass away unless I drink it, may Your will be done."

When He went back to His favorite apostles, again their eyes were heavy with sleep. They were ashamed and knew not what to say to Him. So He left them and returned a third time to pray. He prayed again in the selfsame words to His Father. And this time the pain of His passion came strikingly before Him. In this hour all the ugliness of every sin that would ever be committed weighed upon His sinless soul. He accepted all the sins as if they had been His. He paid the sinners' guilt. He felt, too, the coming pain of physical torture, all the hurt of so many humiliations, and more than all else, the indifference and ingratitude of so many who in spite of His sufferings would be lost. These sufferings sank so deeply into His soul that Saint Luke tells us He was in an agony and had to struggle as if His very life were ebbing from Him. But He prayed longer and harder. The struggle was so great that He broke out in a sweat of blood which soaked His clothing and trickled to the ground.

His heavenly Father sent an angel, not to remove the chalice, but to encourage Him to drink it to the very bottom. Strength and courage came. Jesus no longer feared His sufferings. He arose and went to His apostles and said, "Sleep on now, and take your rest! Behold, the hour is at hand when the Son of Man will be betrayed into the hands of sinners. Arise, let us go. Behold, he who betrays Me is at hand."

Judas, accompanied by the temple guards and a detachment of Roman troops carrying torches and swords and clubs came from the direction of the garden gate. The traitor had planned that a kiss should be the sign by which they might know Jesus. Judas, then, walked up to Jesus and said, "Hail, Master, and kissed Him."

Jesus said, "Friend, do you betray the Son of Man with a kiss?"

Jesus, knowing what was to happen, went to meet His captors and said, "Who is it you are looking for?"

"Jesus of Nazareth," they answered.

He told them, "I am Jesus of Nazareth." When Jesus had said this they fell back as if overcome by awe and terror.

Again Jesus said, "Whom do you want?"

They said, "Jesus of Nazareth."

Jesus answered, "I have told you I am He." And then pointing to His apostles, Jesus continued, "If, therefore, you seek Me, let these go their way."

His apostles asked excitedly, "Lord, shall we strike with the sword?" Peter, not waiting for a reply, drew his sword and cut off the ear of Malchus, a servant of the chief priests.

Jesus said, "Peter, put your sword back into its scabbard," and He healed the ear of Malchus. Then, still addressing Peter, Jesus continued, "Those who use the sword shall perish with the sword. Shall I not drink the chalice that My Father prepared for Me? Do you doubt that if I call upon My Father that He will send more than twelve legions of angels to My side? But how, then, are the Scriptures to be fulfilled?"

Then in a stern tone He said to the rabble, "You have come to Me as against a robber with swords and clubs to seize Me; and yet when I sat daily in the temple teaching, you did not lay hands on Me. But this is your hour and the power of darkness."

Then the guards pressed forward, laid hands on Jesus and tied Him with a rope. When the apostles saw Jesus roughly seized and tied up like a criminal, they were overcome with terror. They fled from the garden leaving the Master alone, a Victim in the hands of His enemies.

Jesus before Caiphas

The guards brought their Prisoner through the dark desolate streets of the city to Annas, the father-in-law of Caiphas the high priest of the Jewish religion. Annas had no official authority to try a prisoner but out of courtesy to him, Christ was made to bear this additional suffering and humiliation.

Christ in the midst of the guards stood before Annas in quiet dignity. For the moment Annas felt a depraved satisfaction at seeing the great Prophet a prisoner of the Sanhedrin, the Council of the Jewish leaders. After a noticeable hesitancy Annas opened the sham investigation by asking Christ about His disciples and His doctrine.

In the reply, the question about His disciples went unanswered. Regarding His doctrine Christ said, "I have spoken openly to the world; I have always taught in the synagogue and in the temple, where all the Jews gather, and in secret I have said nothing. Why do you question Me? Question those who have heard what I have spoken. These know what I have said."

Christ's calm words surprised and startled this outstanding Jewish leader. The momentary frustration that followed was covered, when an attendant struck Christ across the face with a mailed fist, saying, "Is that the way You answer the high priest?" A murmur of approval came from the assembly and confusion followed. Christ's only reaction was to say, "If I have spoken ill, bear witness to the evil; but if well, why do you strike Me?"

Order was restored but Annas had no desire to have more to do with the Prisoner. He brought the trial to an abrupt end and sent the Prisoner, bound as He was, to his son-in-law, Caiphas, the high priest of the year.

During the early hours of the evening, messengers had been sent to the members of the Sanhedrin to notify them about a special session to be held that very evening. Through forceful direction Caiphas let it be understood that the Prisoner, this hated Prophet, was to die. For the sake of appearance, though, there were to be witnesses. At the promise of bribes, many false witnesses volunteered most willingly. Now that all preliminaries, unlawful though they were, had been duly settled, Caiphas called for the Prisoner.

Christ entered, bound, surrounded by the temple guard, and stood in the midst of the assembled leaders of the people, the chief priests and the Scribes. The opening formalities over, the hearing of the witnesses was begun. One by one they came forward to accuse the Prisoner, but no two statements could be made to agree. Neither did they accuse the Prisoner of an offense serious enough to demand a death sentence. Valuable time was being wasted and the unjust judges who knew that all the charges were false, were at a point of desperation, when two witnesses gave this testimony, "We have heard Him say, 'I will destroy this temple that is made by men's hands, and in three days I will build another, with no hands of men to help.'"

The charge was a serious one and now Caiphas and the whole court felt the sentence of condemnation would follow immediately. Cross examination, however, proved that the witnesses had misquoted and distorted the original statement. It could not be accepted.

Every witness had been used and the court had come to no decision. And during all these accusations Christ remained silent and outwardly unmoved. Caiphas, angered because his plans had failed, and for the moment wondering how he could bring about his evil plan, forgot his dignity and shouted at the Prisoner, "Do You make no reply to the things these witness against You?" But Christ said not a word.

Then Caiphas said, "I adjure You by the living God that You tell us whether You are the Christ, the Son of God?"

This was a demand made upon Him which He could not refuse to answer. It was a demand in the Name of God, made by the highest legal authority of His people.

Our Lord's answer was prompt: "You have said it. I am. I say to you, hereafter, you shall see the Son of Man sitting at the right hand of the Power and coming upon the clouds of heaven."

"He has blasphemed!" shouted the High Priest, tearing his garments. "What further need have we of witnessess? You have heard the blasphemy. What do you say?"

With one voice the judges shouted, "He is guilty of death." Immediately the court adjourned.

The noise of the dismissal was a signal to the guards and whosoever might wish to participate in abusing the condemned Criminal. Insults and blows were rained upon Him. He had no peace all through the hours until early morning. They beat Him, mocked Him and spat into His face. He was blindfolded and struck and asked to prophesy who had struck Him.

The Sanhedrin had the power to condemn to death but not the right to carry out the sentence until it was approved by the Roman governor, who at that time was Pontius Pilate. So, at early dawn, just a few hours after the condemnation, the Jewish Council held a second meeting. The meeting was probably held to pass sentence for a formal condemnation in a legal day-session because the session at night when Christ was condemned, was not legal. Besides, the counsil thought it best to prepare charges upon which there would be agreement among them and which would impress the governor. They knew a religious charge, in the eyes of the Roman governor, would not secure the death sentence for their Prisoner. They decided in their appeal to Pilate, to put aside their charge of blasphemy and make their accusation one which would appear to make Jesus an enemy of the Romans.

Peter Denies Jesus

John 18:15-27

Peter regretted his desertion of His Master in the garden and after his fears were somewhat lessened, his love urged him to follow Him from afar. At first he was denied entrance to the courtyard of the palace, but later another disciple who was known to the servants, secured permission for him to enter.

He had just passed over the threshold when the portress looked sharply at Peter and said, "Are you not one of this Man's disciples?"

Peter was immediately disturbed. In a short and quick retort he denied having been a disciple of Christ. He said, "I am not. I do not know what you are talking about."

Peter moved away into the open-air courtyard around which the palace was built. Grouped around a fire, warming themselves, he found a crowd, attendants of the Sanhedrin and servants of the high priest. Thinking that among these he might learn what was happening to his Master, he joined them. He was there but a few moments when another maidservant drew attention to him and said, "This man also was with Jesus of Nazareth."

This time Peter was still more upset. He denied with an oath and in a positive voice said, "I know not the Man."

Just then Peter heard the first cock crow. He knew how wrong he had been and moved away from the crowd toward the vestibule of the main gate. For the space of an hour Peter was left alone with his guilty thoughts. And then a man, a relative of Malchus whose ear Peter had cut off, heard a woman say to Peter, "You are one of this Man's disciples. You are also a Galilean. I can tell from the way you talk."

The man looking at Peter said, "Surely you are one of them. Did I not see you in the garden?"

This time Peter was beside himself with fear. Uttering oaths and curses he denied that he ever knew Christ.

There was a sudden stir in the crowd and all eyes turned toward the guards who were leading their Prisoner across the courtyard. Peter looked, too. His eyes met those of Jesus. Burning sorrow filled Peter's heart and as he hurried away he heard in the distance the sound of a rooster crowing. Peter burst into tears.

JESUS BEFORE PILATE

John 18:28-19, 16

Early Friday morning an order came from Caiphas to the prison guards to start the march with their Prisoner across the city to the prætorium as Pilate's court was called. Most of the members of the Sanhedrin followed, determined in mind to have their way about this disturbing Prophet. Their hope was to get this affair with Pilate over quickly and quietly before the populace would become aware of their plans. They were completely wrong. From all parts of the city friend and foe joined the crowd to learn what would happen to this Man Who, up to now, had kept out of the hands of those who bore such hate toward Him. Would He escape their wiles as He had so often done? Were the chief priests sure of their Victim this time?

Pilate was awaiting them even though it was at an unusually early hour, but his mood was not at all a pleasant one. The Sanhedrin refused to enter the pagan residence for fear of breaking a religious law which forbade entering the house of a Gentile on a feast day, but Jesus was taken within the palace to the Judgment Hall. At this point the Roman soldiers took the place of the temple guard. Pilate conducted the trial from a balcony which overlooked the street. He asked, "What accusation do you bring against this Man?"

Caiphas and his associates were provoked. They answered curtly, "If He were not a malefactor we should not have brought Him to you."

Pilate answered, "Take Him yourself and judge Him according to your Law."

Their reply revealed the end they had in view regarding Jesus. "It is not lawful for us to put anyone to death." And then they brought up the political accusations they had planned to allege against Jesus. "We have found this Man perverting the nation and forbidding the payment of taxes to Cæsar and saying that He is Christ, the King."

This Man a King? The statement surprised Pilate. Going back into the palace, Pilate summoned Jesus. "Are You King of the Jews?" he asked.

As a representative of Rome, Pilate was obliged to take note of these accusations and Jesus responded to his question. He said, "Do you say this of your own accord or is it what others have told you of Me?"

Pilate answered, "Am I a Jew? Your own people and the chief priests have delivered You to me. What have You done?"

Jesus responded to Pilate's first question. He admitted that He was a King and then explained the difference between His kingdom and the kingdoms of the world. "If My kingdom were of this world, My followers would have fought that I might not be delivered to the Jews. My kingdom is not from here."

"You are a King then?" asked Pilate.

"You have said it; I am a King. This is why I have come into the world to bear witness to the truth. Everyone who is of the truth hears My voice."

Pilate was not interested in truth. He replied mockingly, "What is truth?" And, not waiting for an answer, went back to the balcony to tell the Jews, "I find no guilt in this Man."

Had Pilate been a strong and a just judge, having admitted the innocence of Jesus, he should have released Him. But he feared these leaders of the Jewish people might make trouble for him in Rome. His favor with Tiberius, the Emperor, meant more to him than justice.

The council continued its accusation, but Jesus remained silent. They made an accusation of which Pilate took notice. They said, "This man arouses seditions among the people; He has gone around the whole of Judea preaching, beginning from Galilee to this place."

When Galilee was mentioned, Pilate inquired whether Jesus was a Galilean. On learning that He was, he sent Him to Herod for judgment.

Herod, the son of the king who had tried to get Jesus killed as a baby, had been anxious for a long time to see this Wonderworker and was delighted that Pilate had thought to send Him to his court. Surely, now he himself would witness some supernatural incident. But Jesus worked no miracle at Herod's court. He kept a mysterious and embarrassing silence. Angered and

287

Jesus before Pilate

chagrined, Herod and his court made a mockery of Christ and returned Him to Pilate dressed in the garment of a fool.

Again the responsibility to make a decision in this case was Pilate's. He called together the chief priests and magistrates and said, "You have brought before me this Man as one Who perverts the people, and behold, I, upon examining Him in your presence, have found no guilt in Him. Neither has Herod." Then in order to give some satisfaction to the Jews whom he feared, he concluded his address with this most unjust statement, "I will, therefore, scourge Him and release Him."

Each year during the Passover it was the custom to release a prisoner. Pilate arranged a choice between Jesus and a notorious criminal named Barabbas, a murderer and a dangerous malefactor. Pilate was certain that now Jesus would be released. He announced to the crowd: "You have a custom that I should release a prisoner to you at the Passover. Whom do you wish that I should release to you, Barabbas or Jesus who is called the Christ?"

There was a short interval after the announcement. A message from Claudia, Pilate's wife, was delivered: "Have nothing to do with this just Man, for I have suffered many things in a dream today because of Him."

The message encouraged Pilate in his efforts to release Jesus. In the meantime, the chief priests and leaders and servants of the Sanhedrin used this unfortunate interruption for their evil end. Quickly they moved about in the crowd persuading the populace to call for the release of Barabbas. When Pilate, then, repeated his question, "Which of the two do you wish that I release to you?" the crowd shouted, "Barabbas! Give us Barabbas!" Pilate's strategy had failed.

In desperation the Procurator shouted at the crowd: "What shall I do with Jesus Who is called the Christ?"

A wild cry went up, "Crucify Him! Crucify Him!"

Pilate said, "Why, what evil has He done?"

But they cried all the more saying, "Let Him be crucified."

Now Pilate, seeing that he was doing no good, but rather that a riot was breaking out, took water and washed

Jesus Is Scourged

his hands in sight of the crowd, saying, "I am innocent of the blood of this just Man; see to it yourselves."

And all the people answered and said, "His blood be upon us and upon our children."

Reluctantly Pilate released Barabbas and ordered Jesus to be scourged.

JESUS IS SCOURGED

John 19:1-3

Scourging, with the Romans, was a prelude to crucifixion. In scourging, the Jews limited the number of lashes to forty, less one, and it was given with a whip made of three plain strips of leather. The Roman method, however, was a cruel torture compared with that of the Jews. Their whips were made of long, hard thongs studded with bone or bits of metal. There was no stated number of thongs to a whip, and the number of lashes given was left to the decision of the executioners. Since Jesus suffered under Roman command it cannot be determined how many lashes He received. His scourging was an inhuman suffering.

The pitiable condition to which Jesus was reduced by the scourging aroused no sympathy in the soldiers. One of them proposed a mock coronation for this would-be-King. There was hilarious consent. The intention of the crowning was not to inflict more pain—even though it did—but rather to scoff and mock Jesus.

They brought Him from the paved outer court to an inner court where the barracks were placed, and only off-duty soldiers of the cohort would be present. A purple garment, very likely a cast-off scarlet cloak, was thrown about His shoulders, representing the royal purple of a king. A crown was hastily made out of small branches that had long, slender spikes. This was pressed with force on Christ's head. For a scepter they placed a reed in His hand. Then they filed past Him, genuflecting and saying, "Hail, King of the Jews." They took the reed from His hand and hit Him about the head; they spat at Him and jeered at Him.

291

Behold the Man

John 19:4-16

Pilate was still troubled. He wanted to release Jesus if he could, but without any cost to himself. He tried a new means to gain his end. After the scourging and crowning, Jesus was a pitiable sight in the purple robe of mockery with a reed in His hand. The governor would show Him to the people. Pilate did not for an instant doubt that the appearance of Jesus would move all hearts to compassion. He brought Him to the balcony and said, "Behold the Man," as if to say, "Look at the condition of this prisoner and have pity on Him."

But in the chief priests and the guards and in many of the people, too, the appearance of Jesus excited a diabolical hate. In anger and frenzy they cried out, "Crucify Him. Crucify Him."

Pilate knowing they had no reason to do so, answered with a sneer, "Take Him and crucify Him. I find no cause in Him."

The priests were growing weary of trying to get Pilate to pass the sentence of crucifixion on their Prisoner. As another desperate effort they now turned back to their first reason for putting Him to death, blasphemy. They cried, "He has blasphemed. He made Himself the Son of God."

All through the trial Jesus had impressed Pilate. He had never before seen a prisoner accept false accusations and endure ridicule, contempt and every kind of suffering with such patience, fortitude and silence as did this Man. Now when he heard that Jesus claimed to be the Son of God, he was filled with superstitious fear. He took Jesus aside and said, "From where have You come?"

Jesus gave him no answer. Pilate continued, "Why do You not speak to me? Do You not know that I have power to crucify You and I have power to release You?"

Jesus answered, "You would have no power against Me, unless it were given you from above. Therefore, he who has delivered Me to you has committed the greater sin."

The insistent cry of the Jews for Christ's crucifixion weakened Pilate's desire to save Him. He delivered Him to the Jews to be crucified.

On the Road to Calvary

John 19:17-24

The execution of the sentence was carried out at once. Soldiers took the purple cloak from Jesus and gave Him His own garments. With great love Jesus accepted the heavy load of the rough cross. It meant torture and death, but it also meant doing the will of His heavenly Father and the saving of the souls of men. Almost tenderly Jesus put it on His shoulders.

The way to Calvary was cleared by a trumpeter who marched on ahead. Leading the procession was a centurion responsible for carrying out the sentence. He was mounted on a horse and followed by a detachment of foot soldiers. Members of the council pressed on behind Jesus and the two thieves who were to be crucified with Him. The satanic hatred of the members of the council urged them to witness to the bitter end, the sufferings of their innocent Victim. Bringing up the rear was a large crowd of spectators eager to be present at the bloody spectacle of the crucifixion.

The distance to Calvary's hill was short. The first stretch was down into a valley, followed by a steep climb to the top. Jesus was very weak and the burden of the cross too much, so that He fell several times. The soldiers, fearing their Prisoner might die on the way, ordered a passerby to carry the cross. He was Simon of Cyrene, the father of Alexander and Rufus. At first Simon carried the Criminal's cross unwillingly, but as he walked on, enlightenment must have been given him, because in the end he bore it with sympathy and love.

Not all who witnessed this mournful procession showed hatred toward this Man of Sorrows. Women along the road wept without shame or fear. Jesus stopped and spoke to them. He said, "Daughters of Jerusalem, do not weep for Me, but for yourselves and for your children." He added prophetic words which told the destruction that was to come upon Jerusalem, and the sufferings that many of the people, who were in it now, would have to endure because Jerusalem remained wilfully blind to the loving visitation of her God.

Passing through the gate, the procession came to the hill which Jesus climbed slowly and painfully. The hour of the crucifixion was at hand.

Jesus Dies on the Cross

John 19:25-37

When the condemned men reached the top of the hill they were offered a cup of wine mixed with a substance called myrrh which acted as a drug and deadened the sense of pain, but Jesus refused it. The victims were then stripped. And now came the awful moment. Jesus was stretched upon the cross and the hands that had always blessed and the feet that walked the roads of Palestine to bring peace and joy, were nailed with heavy blows to the hard wood of the cross. A wooden tablet bearing the inscription "Jesus of Nazareth, King of the Jews" was fastened above His head. His cross and those of the two thieves were then raised upright and settled down with a jolt into the holes which had been made for them. Christ hung between heaven and earth with thieves to His right and left.

When at last the Scribes and the Pharisees and the leaders saw Jesus secure on the shameful gibbet and suffering His death-agony, they were satisfied. As the soldiers finished their work and moved to a distance, the leaders and rabble moved toward the cross and in boastful, discordant jeers cried out, "If you are the Christ, the Son of God, come down from the cross." "Destroy the temple and in three days build it up again." "He saved others, Himself He cannot save."

Jesus, looking from the scoffing mob to the heavens, called to His Father in mercy, "Father, forgive them, for they know not what they are doing."

The crucified thieves joined the mob in ridicule against their Fellow-Sufferer. But the thief to the right of Jesus was finally impressed with the patience and forgiveness of this so-called "King," and touched by grace, asked Jesus to remember him in His kingdom. Jesus promised not only a remembrance but paradise itself that very day.

At noon a darkness began to spread over the earth. Little by little the scoffers became quiet and moved away. Some went, striking their breasts. A stillness settled on Calvary. The Blessed Mother and Saint John and the other women had been standing beyond, away from the

297

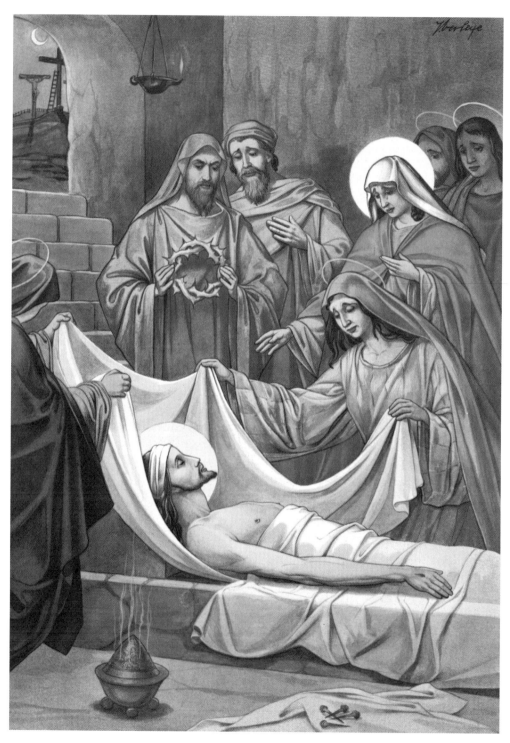

The Burial

rabble. Now they came and stood beneath the cross. When Jesus saw His mother He said, "Woman, behold your Son," and to John, "Son, behold your mother."

Later, in the midst of His awful agony a cry of anguish broke the silence. Jesus said, "My God, My God, why have You forsaken Me?"

After three hours, when Jesus knew His sufferings were at an end and His great work of Redemption was achieved, He said, "It is finished." Crying with a loud voice, He added, "Father, into Your hands I commend My spirit."

Then bowing His head, He died. He finished the bloody but triumphant Sacrifice of Calvary.

THE BURIAL

Luke 23:50-56

When Jesus bowed His head and died, the hour of the power of darkness was at an end. Before death, His enemies, through hate, worked evil upon Him. After death light dawned. Goodness, love and joy were at work.

Joseph of Arimathea, a man of great wealth and a member of the Sanhedrin but not of their spirit, had been among Christ's secret disciples. Fear of the Jews no longer possessed him. He made his way to Pilate's palace and boldly asked for the body of Jesus. There was also Nicodemus, a Doctor of the Law, who had come to Jesus by night for fear of losing his reputation among his associates. In this great hour only love prevailed. They, together with a few other faithful disciples, attended to the burial.

The sacred body was removed from the cross before sunset, the beginning of the Sabbath. Climbing ladders set against the cross, these men gently removed the nails from the hands and feet, and with ropes brought their sacred burden to earth again. Tenderly they drew the long thorns from His sacred head. The rigid body, all covered with dried blood and deep wounds, was carefully washed and sprinkled with a mixture of myrrh and

The Resurrection

aloes which Nicodemus had purchased. It was then carefully wrapped in a linen burial robe. The Blessed Mother, and the holy women looked on with sorrowful but grateful hearts.

Then a quiet procession moved toward the sepulchre which was in a garden close-by. The sepulchre belonged to Joseph of Arimathea. It had been hewn out of solid rock and had never been used. The sacred remains were carried through the opening and down a few steps into a small vestibule. Here the women remained while the men brought their burden into an inner chamber and placed it on a stone couch. The head was wrapped in a large linen cloth. Powdered spices were sprinkled over the outer covering and around in the tomb. After these ceremonies, all left, and the great circular stone was rolled into its place before the entrance.

The Blessed Mother was sorrowful but not distracted with grief. There was peace and calm and great expectation in her heart. Mary believed and understood as no one else did, that the hour of the glorious Resurrection was nearing.

THE RESURRECTION

Luke 24:1-11

The tomb was closed late Friday afternoon which for the Jews was practically the dawn of the Sabbath. During this time the apostles who had fled in fear when Jesus had been made prisoner, found refuge and security behind locked doors in the Cenacle, the upper room, where they had eaten the Last Supper. There, too, later, they were joined by Mary and John and Mary Magdalen and the other holy women. Mary was now their support and hope. Her understanding gave them comfort. In the presence of this valiant woman their love for and their faith in the Master was re-awakened. But Mary kept the secret of her own faith in the immediate Resurrection of her Son. In His own way, He Himself would reveal the great mystery to His beloved disciples.

301

Another group gathered togother but in an entirely opposite mood. The Scribes and the Pharisees left Calvary with a feeling of great satisfaction. The Prophet of Nazareth was dead and buried, and His little band of followers scattered. These men of the Law were grateful now that they had thought early in the day to keep themselves from defilement. Now they could partake of the holy Paschal celebration with joy and peace of mind.

But by Saturday evening joy and peace gave way to anxiety. Caiphas began to feel uneasy. He reasoned within himself: "Two of our own associates, Joseph of Arimathea and Nicodemus, are already in league with the followers of this Man and the body of this "criminal" is in Joseph's own tomb. They and the disciples might hide the body and spread the rumor that the prophecy of the Resurrection has come true." Caiphas lost no time in reaching Pilate. He explained his fears and asked that the tomb be safely guarded. Pilate let it be understood that if there was to be a guard, it would have to be their own. So Caiphas arranged that Israel's seal be set on the tomb and that a guard remain there on duty for three days and three nights.

At the break of dawn, the first day of the week, there was a great earthquake, for an angel of the Lord, in human form, came down from heaven and rolled back the stone from the tomb and sat upon it. His countenance was like lightning and his garments like snow. The guards were terrified and became like dead men. As soon as they regained power to move, they hurried from the tomb and ran to the city to report their experience.

Caiphas was much disturbed. He hurriedly called a special assembly of the chief priests and leaders. Although dead, this Nazarene seemed to have powers beyond their control. There was much discussion until they agreed finally to bribe the guards to say that while they, the guards, had fallen asleep during the night, the disciples of Christ came and stole the body.

The holy women had spent the Sabbath in the Cenacle, impatient to get back to the sepulchre where the Master's body lay. The burial on Friday had been done in haste and they wished to complete the anointing. So, when it was yet dark, Mary Magdalen, and Mary, the mother of James and Joseph, and the other holy women, laden with spices, set out for the tomb.

As they hurried on, they suddenly remembered the large stone that had been placed before the tomb and wondered what they would do. Although they knew they could not move it, they continued on their way. How surprised they were to find the stone already rolled back! Mary Magdalen was immediately distressed, and suspecting that the body of her Lord had been stolen, did not wait to enter the tomb, but turned back in great haste to the Cenacle. There, gasping for breath, she explained to Peter and John, "They have taken the body from the tomb and we do not know where they have laid Him."

Meanwhile the other women entered the tomb. They were frightened at seeing a young man clothed in white, sitting at the right side of the tomb. He said to them, "Do not be afraid. You are looking for Jesus of Nazareth, Who was crucified. He is risen, He is not here. Behold the place where they laid Him. But go tell His disciples and Peter that He goes before you into Galilee. There you shall see Him as He told you."

With no loss of time these holy women obeyed the message of the angel. In fear, but with the joy of bearing good news, they returned to the Cenacle and delivered their message, but it was received as an impossible tale and no one believed them.

Magdalen's story, however, brought action. Peter and John ran to the tomb. John outran Peter, but waited outside the tomb until Peter arrived. Both went into the sepulchre. They saw the linen cloths lying there and the head-piece folded. Peter knew at once that there had been no robbery and John "saw and believed." But, "Peter... went away wondering to himself at what had come to pass."

But Mary Magdalen, alone, stood outside weeping, at the tomb. As she wept, she entered the inner chamber to look once more at the place where Jesus' body had been laid. The place was not empty, as she had thought. There were present two angels in white sitting, one at the head and one at the feet, where the body of Christ had been laid. The heavenly visitors asked, "Woman, why are you weeping?"

She replied, "Because they have taken away my Lord and I do not know where they have laid Him."

The Two Disciples

In her anxiety to find the body somewhere, she looked about and saw a Man standing outside the tomb. He, too, questioned her, "Woman, why are you weeping? Whom do you seek?"

Believing that the Man might be a gardener employed in the garden in which the tomb was, she said to Him, "Sir, if you have removed Him, tell me where you have laid Him and I will take Him away."

Instead of giving a direct reply, the Stranger looked at her and called her by her name, "Mary!"

Immediately grief and sorrow gave way to deepest joy. Recognizing His voice, she fell at Christ's feet and with a great burst of love cried, "Rabboni, Master!"

In a desire never to lose Him again, she made an effort to embrace His feet, but Jesus said to her gently, "Do not touch Me; for I am not yet ascended to My Father. But go to My brethren and say to them, 'I ascend to My Father and to your Father, to My God and to your God.'"

Mary Magdalen ran to the Cenacle to announce the good message to the disciples, but they were still unbelieving. "And they, hearing that He was alive and had been seen by her, did not believe."

THE TWO DISCIPLES

Luke 24:13-35

Cleophas, one of the disciples, with a companion left the Cenacle, to return to Emmaus. They were discouraged and thought that their hopes regarding Christ were at an end. As they walked along talking over the things that had happened, they were conscious of a footfall close behind them. Because of the circumstances, they were somewhat uneasy about meeting a stranger. When this Man reached them, He opened conversation saying, "What words are these you are having one with the other as you walk on your way and why are you sad?"

Cleophas asked, "Are You the only stranger in the city who does not know the things that have happened during these days?"

Jesus Appears to His Apostles

It was Jesus to Whom they were speaking, but He hid His identity from them and asked, "What things?" They answered, "Concerning Jesus of Nazareth, Who was a Prophet, mighty in work and word before God and all the people and how our chief priests and rulers delivered Him up to be sentenced to death, and crucified Him. But we were hoping that it would be He Who would redeem Israel. Besides, this is the third day since these things happened."

"It is true," they added, "certain women of our company, who were at the tomb, astounded us. They came saying that they had seen a vision of angels who said that He is alive. Some of our company went to the tomb and found it as the women had said, but, Him they did not see."

Then, beginning at Moses and all the prophets, this "Stranger" explained to them what was in the Scriptures concerning Him.

As they approached Emmaus, the place where the disciples were stopping, the Stranger made as if He were going on. The disciples, however, pressed the Traveler to remain with them.

Later as they sat at table and the Stranger took bread and blessed and broke and began handing it to them, their eyes were opened. It was Jesus. But in the moment of recognition He vanished from their sight.

Though it was very late, Cleophas and his companion hurried back to the Cenacle to tell the brethren the good news. On the way they said one to the other, "Was not our heart burning within us while He spoke?"

JESUS APPEARS TO HIS APOSTLES

John 21:19-23

The two disciples had returned from Emmaus to the Cenacle, and were narrating their experience to those disciples who still doubted the Resurrection, when suddenly, even though the doors of the Cenacle were barred, Jesus stood in their midst. He said, "Peace be to you! It is I; fear not."

All were filled with terror, disturbed because their Visitor seeming to have flesh and blood, came through the barred doors. They looked upon Him as a ghost or a vision. Jesus said, "Why are you disturbed? Why do thoughts arise in your minds? See My hands and My feet that It is I, Myself."

Even though they saw Jesus before them and were filled with joy to see Him, doubt was still in their minds.

To make them realize that It was He Himself and not a ghost or a vision, He asked, "Have you anything here to eat?"

Wondering, they offered Him a piece of broiled fish and a honeycomb, which He ate before them. Slowly, belief came. It was Jesus!

Then Jesus said to them, "These are the words which I spoke to you while I was yet with you that all things might be fulfilled that were written in the Law of Moses and the Prophets and the Psalms concerning Me."

Again He repeated the salutation, "Peace be to you!" and added, "as the Father has sent Me, I also send you."

When He had said this, He breathed upon them and said, "Receive the Holy Spirit; whose sins you shall forgive, they are forgiven them; and whose sins you shall retain, they are retained."

THOMAS SEES THE RISEN CHRIST

John 21:19-30

Thomas was absent on Easter Sunday evening from the assembly of the apostles at the Cenacle, and when he heard that Christ had appeared in their midst, he would not believe. Possibly Thomas was more discouraged over the recent Passion than were the other disciples. Instead of rejoicing that they had seen the Lord, he sullenly rejected their word that the Crucified had risen. Until Christ appeared again the next Sunday Thomas remained stubborn in his disbelief.

Finally when he saw that his associates firmly believed that they had seen Christ and that He was truly risen from the dead, Thomas gave his own demands for believing. He said, "Unless I see in His hands the print of the nails, and put my finger into the place of the nails, and put my hand into His side, I will not believe."

"And after eight days, His disciples were again inside, and Thomas with them. Jesus came, the doors being closed, and stood in their midst, and said, 'Peace be to you!' Then He said to Thomas, 'Bring here your finger, and see My hands; and bring here your hand, and put it into My side; and be not unbelieving, but believing.'"

Overwhelmed, Thomas no longer doubted. He fell on his knees before His risen Christ and made the most forceful act of faith given in the Gospels. He cried, "My Lord and My God!"

Christ pardoned Thomas' want of faith but gave him a reprimand: "Because you have seen Me, Thomas, you believe, but blessed are they who have not seen and yet believe."

During the forty days between Christ's Resurrection and His Ascension He appeared many times to His apostles and sometimes, too, to those who were His faithful followers. He consoled, comforted and instructed them. He went before them into Galilee as He had prophesied. On the shores of the lake He gave Peter the occasion to make public atonement for his threefold denial and to profess his great love for Him. Jesus did not only forgive Peter, but also carried out His promise of making him the supreme pastor of His Church. "Feed My lambs; feed My sheep." On the mountain side in Galilee He gave the apostles the great command to teach all nations, promising to be with them to the end of the world.

The Ascension

Acts 1

After Christ had shown His disciples by many proofs that He was still alive after the Passion and Death, and when the forty days His Father had willed that He remain with them had come to an end, it was necessary that He depart from them. He was now to go to the Father to receive the reward of His victory.

He invited them to a last meal with Him. While they sat at table, He instructed them not to leave Jerusalem because it was here that the promise of the Father would be fulfilled. The Holy Spirit, the Comforter, would come upon them. "For John indeed baptized with water, but you shall be baptized with the Holy Spirit not many days from now."

They knew that Jesus was giving them His final message, yet, even in this last talk, they showed again that their minds were still turned toward an earthly kingdom. "Lord," they asked, "are You at this time going to restore the kingdom to Israel?"

Jesus did not try to change their mistaken notion, but simply said, "It is not for you to know the times or dates which the Father has fixed by His own authority, but you shall receive power when the Holy Spirit comes upon you, and you shall be witnesses for Me in Jerusalem and in all Judea and Samaria and even to the very ends of the earth."

When He had said this they arose from table, and leaving the city, crossed the brook of Cedron and began to climb the slope of Mount Olivet. Having reached the summit of the hill, Jesus looked upon His beloved disciples, raised His hands in blessings and as they watched, visibly, in the presence of the whole assembly of followers, arose slowly and majestically in the air.

While they stood spellbound looking up toward heaven, a cloud hid Jesus from their eyes. But they still continued to gaze, when... "Behold two men stood by them in white garments, and said to them, 'Men of Galilee, why do you stand looking up to heaven? This Jesus Who has been taken up from you into heaven, will come in the same way as you have seen Him going up to heaven.'"

Then, with hearts full of joy at the triumph of their Master they went back to Jerusalem to await the promise of the Holy Spirit.

Acts 2

The message of the angels brought the apostles back to things of earth. They followed the in- struction they had received from Jesus, and re- turned to Jerusalem to the shelter of the Cenacle. Saint Luke in the Acts of the Apostles says, "Coming into the city, they went up into the upper room where they dwelt, Peter and John, James and Andrew, Philip and Thomas, Bartholomew and Matthew, James the son of Alpheus and Simon the Zealot, and Judas the brother of James. All these with one mind, gave themselves up to prayer, with Mary, the Mother of Jesus, and the rest of the women and all the brethren."

Peter stood up and spoke to them. The company numbered one hundred twenty. "Brethren, the Scriptures must be fulfilled which the Holy Spirit declared before by the lips of David about Judas, who showed the way to the men that arrested Jesus. He had been one of us and had his share in the ministry... and his ministry, let another take."

So, Peter suggested that they select one of their number to become a witness with them of the Resurrec- tion of Christ. He recommended that the choice should fall on one who was in their company all the time that the Lord moved among them, from John's baptism until the day of the Ascension. Two names were put forward, Joseph called Barsabbas, who was surnamed Justus, and Matthias. Peter and all present prayed, "Lord, You know the hearts of all men, show us which of these two You have chosen to take his place in the work of the apostle- ship, from which Judas has fallen away and gone to the place which belonged to him."

They cast lots and the lot fell upon Matthias and he took rank with the eleven apostles.

From the day of the Ascension until Pentecost, ten days, this group of Christ's disciples, under the direc- tion of Peter and the Mother of Christ, remained together in prayer.

"Suddenly, at dawn of Pentecost, a sound came from Heaven like that of a strong wind blowing and filled the house where they were sitting. And there appeared to them what seemed to be tongues of fire, which parted and came to rest on each of them. And they were filled with the Holy Spirit and began to speak in strange languages, even as the Holy Spirit prompted them to speak."

In Jerusalem at this time were many devout Jews from every nation under the sun. These, too, heard the sound of the mighty wind and gathered around the Cenacle, wondering what had taken place.

The Holy Spirit had now been given to the disciples, and the Catholic Church was brought into being. Immediately the apostolic work was begun. All who had persevered in prayer in the Cenacle and had received the Holy Spirit came forth and moved into the street. Possibly they were making their way to the temple to give thanks to God. Fear had gone; all were inspired. Each felt a desire to spread the good news of the Redemption.

The multitude listening to these first bearers of "good news" was bewildered in mind because each heard them speaking in his own language. They said, "Are these not all Galileans? And how is it that we each hear them in our own language?" They asked one another, "What can this mean?"

There were some who said mockingly, "They have had their fill of new wine."

Peter, with the eleven standing beside him, lifted up his voice and spoke to the multitude. He urged the people to listen to his message. He told them that he and his brethren were not drunk as some supposed, but the words of the prophet Joel had been fulfilled that the Holy Spirit would be poured forth.

Then, fearlessly, Peter spoke of Jesus Christ: a Man approved by God, Who by miracles, wonders and signs proved that He was the Son of God. "Him," he told them, "you have put to death. By God's merciful plan and foreknowledge, you, through the hands of wicked men, have crucified Him. But God has raised Him up. We are

The Descent of the Holy Spirit

witnesses of it. Let all the house of Israel know that Jesus is Lord and Messias and reigns in Heaven."

Many hearing Peter's words acknowledged their mistake and asked what they should do. Peter told them to repent and be baptized in the name of Jesus Christ, to have their sins forgiven. And he said, "Then you will receive the Holy Spirit. This promise is for you and your children and for all those, however far away, whom Our Lord calls to Himself." Peter told these believing people to save themselves from a false-minded generation.

That day three thousand souls were baptized. These with the one hundred twenty disciples formed the first members of the Catholic Church. And immediately they began to live a community life under the leadership of Peter and the apostles.

The apostles were especially inspired. They were no longer men, fearful and wanting in courage. They were unconquerable. They preached Jesus and Jesus crucified. Suffering, imprisonment, banishment and even death lost their fears for these valiant men. Rather, these things encouraged their zeal. This miraculous change was brought about by the Holy Spirit working in the way Our Lord had foretold.

With the descent of the Holy Spirit, the Catholic Church had begun and would continue to exist in a continuous and strong growth forever. Surprisingly on the first day of the new Church, which was but fifty days after Christ had been spurned and mocked and crucified, three thousand rallied to His cause. After the miraculous cure of the cripple near the Beautiful Gate, a few thousand more were added to this first beginning of faithful souls.

At this time, because of the Jewish Pentecost, Jerusalem was crowded. After the feast, these pilgrims, returning to distant parts, prepared the way for the apostles by telling of the wonderful events which had taken place in Jerusalem.

Organization began at once. A strange and fearless zeal took possession of the apostles and this new sect. Boldly Peter preached the greatness and glory of the Christ Whom these people had dared to crucify. In spite of ridicule, opposition and persecution, preaching by the apostles and these ardent converts never ceased.

For awhile the apostles remained in Jerusalem and its surroundings but later with many of their converts they moved from these narrow limits and brought the new and wonderful message of Christ's teaching through all Judea, Galilee and Samaria; and then to wider circles, Phoenicia, Cyprus and Antioch. In every place their message bore rich fruits. Everywhere new centers sprang up.

Paul, the greatest convert of all times, added his powerful influence. His missionary journeys among the Gentiles brought thousands into this new Church. He spent thirty years in labor, suffering and persecution to spread the message of Christ's teaching and love.

According to God's plan, faith in Christ spread and many churches were founded all over the world of that day. Rome at that time was a general meeting place for all nationalities and creeds. The Church which was begun there, from its very start had a singular influence. It may be that Saint Peter had been its founder for history tells us that he labored there and also died there. After Peter came to live in Rome, this Church, by its strong union in sympathy and direction to all other Churches which had been established, made true the prophecy of Christ: "And I say to you, you are Peter, and upon this rock I will build My Church, and the gates of hell shall not prevail against it. And I will give you the keys of the kingdom of heaven and whatever you shall bind on earth shall be bound in heaven, and whatever you shall loose on earth shall be loosed in heaven."

Peter's authority was looked upon as infallible from the very beginning because of Christ's commission to him. Peter's voice prevailed. It was the authoritative, the supreme voice of the Church. This absolute authority was passed on to every legitimate Pope from Peter down to our present Holy Father. God was with His Church and would remain with it forever.

The Church lived on although through all ages she has ever been attacked both from within and without. She has lived through hundreds of bitter persecutions. Individuals, often great leaders in the Church, questioned her divine right and sacred claims and sometimes dragged whole peoples away from her. Secular states denied her legal rights and earthly estates were taken from her, but the Church remained. At all times it was defended by her own noble leaders and scholars and enriched through the eminent lives of her many saints. This Church at Rome, known as Saint Peter's of Rome, grew into a spiritual world power.

We must not look upon the Church as a strong fortress of countless churches—large and beautiful and some just small shacks—in every land under the sun. These buildings, venerable as they are, merely house the Church. The Church's strength is not in wood or stone. It lives deep in the heart of every faithful Catholic. This living faith is the gift of spiritual life flowing directly from the fountain of eternal life which is God Himself. Each individual soul blessed with this life is free to continue to live it or give it up, but no power on earth can take it away from him.

This spiritual life is possessed by the Church under different forms. It comes to us through the Church's Sacramental life. This life brings grace at the dawn of our natural life or later, and again when death is near. This sacramental life of grace brings us forgiveness of sin; power and strength to resist evil. It supplies the sacred food that nourishes our souls. The Sacrament of Matrimony gives grace to married couples that they may live happily and bring up their children as good sons and daughters of our Catholic Church.

The Church's sacrificial life stems from the Sacrament of Holy Orders and regulates above all else the Sacrificial Offering, Holy Mass. Hourly, by day and night throughout the world, this great Sacrifice is being offered and gives worship, glory and thanks to God. The hierarchy of the Church, the bishops and priests, carefully preserve the truth of Christ's teaching and are the good shepherds of His faithful people. Their work of spreading Christ's teaching is never at an end.

The Church will ever go on; she will abide forever. In heaven, the faithful are known as the Church Triumphant. On earth, the faithful still fighting to reach heaven make up the Militant Church. The Suffering Church is made up of the souls departed who were not pure enough to enter heaven. Both the Church on earth and God's saints remember and pray for the Suffering Church. They in turn pray for the members still trying to reach heaven. This union of the faithful in heaven, on earth and in purgatory is called the Communion of Saints.

There are many other phases or ways to look at the Church but because it is a divine work, we will never fully understand its power and beauty. But this we know. God has left divine truth with His Church. She has kept it pure and free from error. If we follow the Church, therefore, we can know for a certainty that we are on the path of heaven.

318   The Catholic Church is your legacy from God.

NINIVE

HARAN

TIGRIS RIVER

BABYLONE

EUPHRATES RIVER

ARABIA

UR

OLD TESTAMENT WORLD

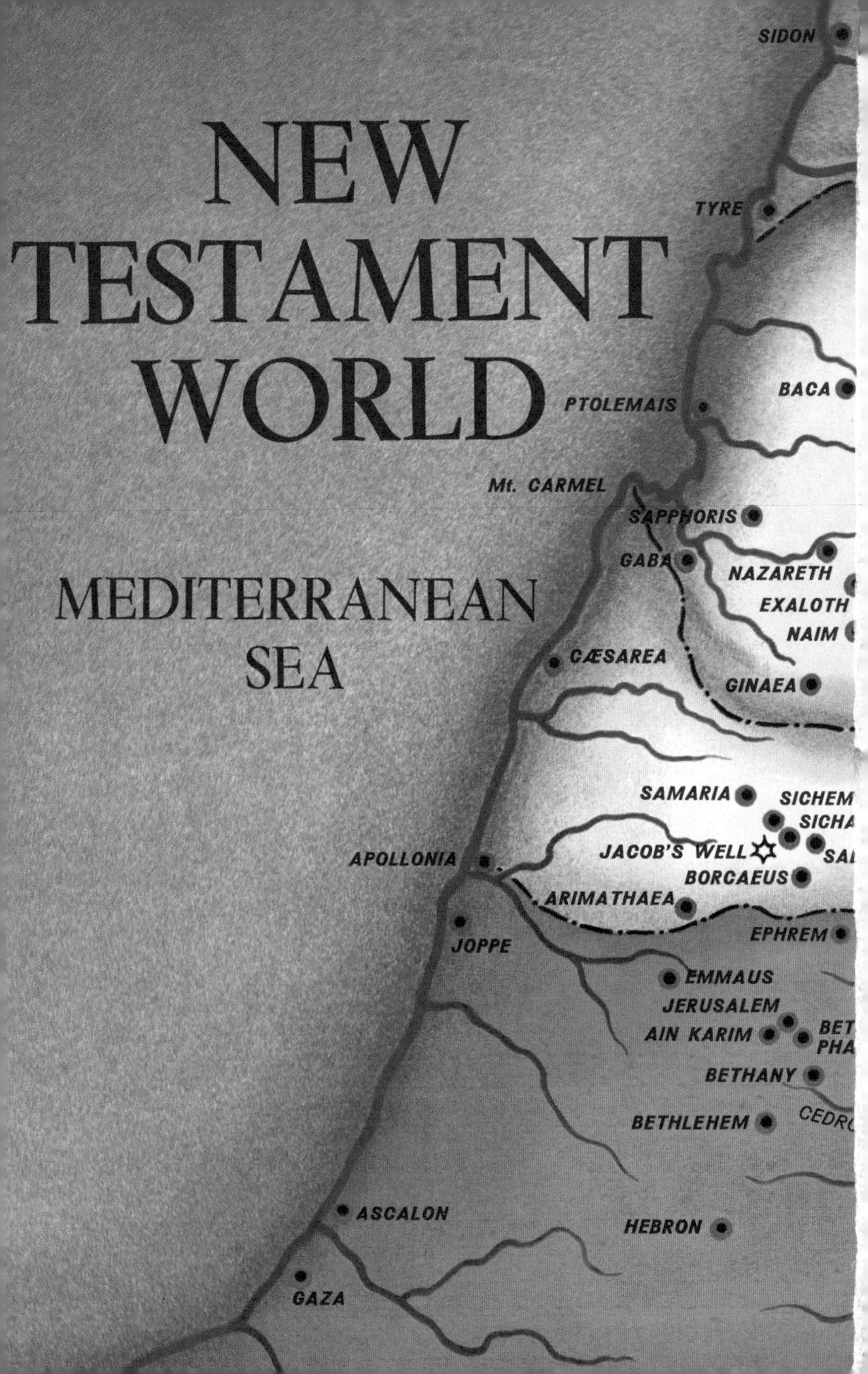

NEW TESTAMENT WORLD

MEDITERRANEAN SEA

SIDON

TYRE

BACA

PTOLEMAIS

Mt. CARMEL

SAPPHORIS

GABA

NAZARETH

EXALOTH

NAIM

CÆSAREA

GINAEA

SAMARIA

SICHEM

SICHA

APOLLONIA

JACOB'S WELL ✡

SAL

BORCAEUS

ARIMATHAEA

EPHREM

JOPPE

EMMAUS

JERUSALEM

AIN KARIM

BET

PHA

BETHANY

BETHLEHEM

CEDR

ASCALON

HEBRON

GAZA

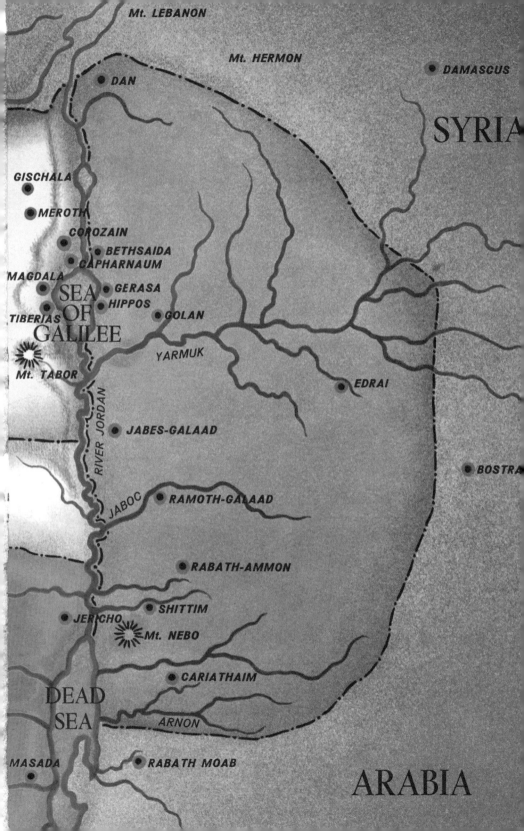

St.MARK

St.MATTHEW